HEROES OF THE CROSS

Heroes of the Cross

DR. FREDERICK BAEDEKER
:: HORACE UNDERWOOD ::
ARTHUR NEVE OF KASHMIR

Christine I. Tinling

Schmul Publishing Co., Inc.
Wesleyan Book Club   Salem, Ohio
1984

ISBN 0-88-019-162-7

Printed by
Old Paths Tract Society Inc.
Shoals, Indiana 47581

FREDERICK BAEDEKER THE PRISONERS' FRIEND

ROUND THE WORLD

BAEDEKER! Have you ever heard that name before? Perhaps not. Ask those who have travelled abroad and they will say at once, " Oh, yes, the guide book man! " Try it and see if they don't. His name is so well known that it has almost become a common noun. People speak of taking their Baedeker with them, as they would speak of taking their umbrella or their purse.

Karl Baedeker was a German book-seller and publisher, and he brought out guide-books of different countries till he had described most of the civilised lands of the world. They were packed full of useful information and told you where to go and what to see and what to pay. They were printed in German and French and English and Baedeker thus became famous. His success was due to hard work: he was very careful and exact in all he wrote, and then too, he employed good scholars to help him.

But our story is about another Baedeker, not that one. The guide-book man had a cousin who sometimes wrote for him, and he also became famous, in a different way. Karl was a guide to all parts of the earth and a very good one too : Frederick was to thousands of people a guide to heaven. He showed them the way to God ; he taught them to put their trust in Jesus, who is the Way, the Truth and the Life.

Frederick became known as Doctor Baedeker, because of the letters Ph.D. after his name, which mean " doctor of philosophy " not medicine. But the Russian peasants to whom he afterwards went called him " Dedouchka " or

"Dear Grandfather." In this story I shall use all these names and you can pick out the one you like the best.

But first we must call him Frederick and begin with his boyhood for, of course, it was only long afterwards that he earned his other names.

The little town of Witten, where he was born, is near the river Rhine, which is very beautiful thereabouts. In the Baedeker home there were four boys and two girls, and Frederick was the youngest son but one. They called him Fritz for short. Their father was a naturalist; he studied animals and particularly birds. This was very jolly for the children, for he could tell them no end of interesting things and they could help him hunt for specimens.

Mr. Baedeker had a big collection of birds and their eggs, some of them very rare. There were eggs of different shades and colours, brown and blue and green, pearly white ones and pretty speckled ones. They were all sizes too, from the big eggs of the eagle and the stork down to the tiny ones of the little hedge wren. He knew them all, and the children learned to know them too. Mr. Baedeker was so famous that when people in far away parts of Europe found some egg that they could not name, they would pack it up and send it to him and he would tell them what it was. He wrote a book about birds' eggs and painted the pictures himself. After he died his collection was taken to Berlin and placed in a natural history museum.

Fritz's mother was rather strict, but I expect those four boys needed to be kept in order and perhaps even the girls too. Six children are quite a houseful, and I dare say they made plenty of noise. Fritz was specially fond of his elder sister Pauline, and when he was in trouble it was to her he went.

At sixteen he left school and started in business. When he was twenty-one, however, he had to stop work and go into the army for two years, for in Germany and other European countries the young men are trained as soldiers whether they like it or not. We ought to be thankful it is not so in England.

Fritz's regiment was stationed at Cologne, and while they were there Queen Victoria paid a visit to Germany and he had a glimpse of her and Prince Albert. The streets were grandly decorated and brightly lighted, and everybody seemed glad to welcome the English Queen and her Consort.

Before many years had passed Fritz went over to England and thus began those wanderings which lasted as long as he lived. He was a born traveller : in the first part of his life he travelled to please himself, and in the second he travelled to serve the Lord Jesus.

After he had explored his own country and been to London and looked around there, he decided to sail for Tasmania. I don't know why he chose that island, but if you look at the map you will see it was as far away as he could get, so this may have been the reason. He sailed in a French ship and had plenty of excitement, for they ran into a violent gale and came near being wrecked. After a voyage of 130 days they safely reached port.

Fritz Baedeker was a clever young fellow, and he soon found something to do. He got into a school and then into a college, where he taught French and German until the longing for travel came over him again. He went off to Australia for a couple of years and then at last he felt it was time to return home and see his folks. So he took a boat that was going round Cape Horn and thus got back to Europe. One day he surprised the family by walking in and sitting down in his own old chair, but the joy of the home-coming was spoilt because Pauline was not there. She had died while Fritz was away.

He had some friends in England, people whom he had met in his travels, and he thought he would pop over to see them. But once he got here he could not tear himself away. He liked our country so much that he decided to settle down and become a British subject.

If you have been looking at the map you will have seen what a great traveller young Baedeker was by this time. And this is not half the story. His whole life was full of adventure and the second part was far more thrilling than the first.

THE GREAT DECISION

WHEN Dr. Baedeker settled in England he made his home in the beautiful seaside town of Weston-super-Mare. No doubt you enjoy going to the seaside in the summer and you would perhaps like to live there altogether and be able to play beside the waves and watch the ships the whole year round. The doctor had a pretty home perched on the hillside near the woods and from his windows he could look out over the bay. One tiny islet standing alone was the only land between his house and New York.

He and Mrs. Baedeker (for he was now married) had plenty of friends and many things to make life pleasant. They enjoyed themselves in various ways, but they did not know the greatest happiness of all, for they were not Christians. In fact, Dr. Baedeker went so far as to say he did not believe in God. You will find as you grow older that the reason why some people don't believe in God is because they don't want to believe in Him. If it is true that Jesus died for us, then of course we ought to live for Him and show our gratitude by obedience. I can't tell you exactly what Dr. Baedeker thought and felt : I only know that he did not care to hear about religion and he kept away from the places where it was mentioned.

One day it was announced that a certain Lord Radstock was coming to Weston to speak at several meetings. It seemed rather unusual that a lord should be a preacher, and many people who would not have gone to hear a clergyman or a minister were curious to know what this nobleman would have to say. But Dr. Baedeker was not one of these.

He would certainly have stayed away, but that a neighbour begged him to go. This gentleman had himself just found Jesus as his Saviour and wanted Dr. Baedeker to know Him, too. The Doctor agreed to go just for once, though he was not at all inclined. To his great surprise the talk was quite interesting and he went again and again, always slipping out as quickly as possible when it was over. One night Lord Radstock saw him hurrying away and put his hand on his shoulder and said, " God has a message for you to-night."

It was quite true. That evening the Holy Spirit showed him how wrong he had been, and how he was a sinner and needed a Saviour and the Saviour was ready that minute to receive him and forgive him and make him His own. He knelt down and gave himself then and there to the Lord Jesus. Then he went home and told his wife.

She did not like it at all. Somehow she felt that from now onwards everything would be different and her husband would not care for some of the pleasures they had had together, since he had found another kind. She thought it would be very dull. However, it was not long before she began to see that she might be wrong and she said to herself, " Perhaps I am refusing something I ought to take." Then she also came to Jesus and very soon they were happier than they had ever been in their lives before. They found that there is no pleasure in the world so great as that of serving Him.

God had a great work for Dr. Baedeker to do and as we go on with the story you will see what a wonderful life his became. Thousands of people in different countries of Europe and Asia have had cause to be thankful that ever they met him. His name is greatly honoured and beloved. But if you ask me the name of the man who invited him to that meeting, I shall have to say, " I don't know." The Lord Jesus knows his name and will not fail to reward him for the service he did that day.

IN RUSSIAN PALACES

DR. BAEDEKER spoke several languages and very soon found a use for them in the service of the Lord Jesus. Think of this when you are studying your lessons : it will be easier to master the hard ones if you remember that He may some time want you to use that knowledge.

When visiting in Germany the doctor interpreted for a noted evangelist and he did it so well that people begged him to go about preaching on his own account. Then his friend Lord Radstock said there were many Germans in Russia who never heard the Gospel and asked him to go there for a time.

So Dr. and Mrs. Baedeker let their house and packed their trunks and set out for Russia. They took with them the little girl they had adopted whose name was Emmie.

Russia was quite different in those days from what it is to-day. Now it is a republic of a peculiar kind about which I can't attempt to tell you. Then it was under the Czars or Emperors and at St. Petersburg the capital there was a grand court, to which many noble families belonged.

A certain book held all their names and their family trees for hundreds of years back. It was called the Velvet Book because it was bound in rich crimson velvet. It was kept in one of the offices of the Senate (which is like our House of Lords) and very carefully guarded. People were proud to be included in the Velvet Book. Some rich men would have given anything to have had their names written there. They had made their money in trade and could not boast of noble ancestors, and they schemed and planned in every way possible to get included in the list of grandees, and often it was all in vain.

At the time of our story some of the Russian nobles had just found out that there was another book of far more importance than the Velvet Book. They had been reading the Bible for themselves and learned that those who trust in Jesus belong to God's own royal family, " whose names are in the Book of Life."

One of these was Colonel Paschkoff, who ought really to have a story to himself. Besides his mansion in St. Petersburg, he had lands in several parts of Russia, and he owned some copper mines and altogether was a wealthy man. While he was an officer, loyal and true, in the army of the Czar, he was also a soldier of Jesus Christ and faithful in his allegiance to Him. He used to gather his friends together to study the Bible and he had meetings in his drawing-room for the preaching of the Gospel, and in many ways he tried to bring others to know his Lord.

The Czar Alexander III heard of all this and actually banished him from his native land. It is very hard for us who live in England to imagine what these Russian Christians had to bear, for ours is a free country and we worship God as we see fit, no one daring to make us afraid. It happened that when Dr. and Mrs. Baedeker were in St. Petersburg Colonel Paschkoff wrote to the Czar and asked if he might come home on a little visit and attend to some business. The Czar gave him permission to come for three months, and there was great rejoicing when he arrived. His friends called to see him and they read the Bible together, for there they found comfort in their hard trials. The Czar heard of this : some sneak told him, no doubt, and he sent for the Colonel.

" I hear you have resumed your old practices," he said sternly. " My friends have simply called to see me," the officer replied, " and we have read God's Word and prayed together."

" Which you know I will not permit," said the Czar. " I will not allow you to defy me. If I had thought you would do this, I should not have let you come back at all. Now go, and never set your foot upon Russian soil again."

So this good soldier was exiled for ever from his country because of his faithfulness to Christ.

I don't want you to get the idea that the Czar was against all religion, as unfortunately the Russian rulers are to-day. There were thousands of churches in the country, and there was an army of priests and bishops, and many long services were held, with music and processions and holy water and incense. But when people met quietly to read the Bible and to pray, and when they tried to tell others about Jesus, and how He had saved them and made them happy, the Czar objected to all this and tried to stamp it out.

But he did not succeed. Though he punished some prominent men like Colonel Paschkoff, others went on doing what they thought right just the same. He could not very well interfere with an English visitor like Dr. Baedeker, who had brought introductions from people of note in this country. And you can well understand what a blessing and comfort the doctor was to these Russian Christians who had not often the chance of hearing the Gospel preached.

There was one princess in particular who loved to entertain him and to have meetings for him in her great white drawing-room. Like the Shunammite lady in the Bible, she prepared a prophet's chamber, but it was not so plain as Elisha's. The mantelpiece, the cornices and the pillars were made of that beautiful green stone known as malachite. Later on the Doctor visited the quarries in Siberia from whence it came.

He stayed with ever so many princes and barons and counts in their town mansions or on their beautiful country estates, and they welcomed him as a servant of Christ. St. Paul once said that the people in a certain place were so glad to see him that they treated him as if he had been an angel, and that is how these Russian Christians felt about Dr. Baedeker.

One day a young Count brought his sleigh to meet him at the station and on the way home the sleigh overturned in a snow-drift and the Count and the Doctor were both thrown out with all the luggage on top of them. Happily they were not hurt.

It was glorious to drive mile after mile in the crisp, clear

Dr. Baedeker travelling by sleigh over the snows

air, with the sun shining and the sleigh-bells tinkling and kind friends to give a hearty welcome at the end of the journey. But it was quite easy to lose one's way when the snow covered the roads as well as the fields and made the whole landscape look like a big white blanket. Writing home one day the doctor said they had had four fine horses to pull the sleigh and two men on horseback riding in front to pick out the road for them.

He enjoyed all these good times and the comforts of these wealthy homes, when they happened to come his way. But his heart was not set on such things : all he really cared about was to bring people to the knowledge of the Lord Jesus. He said, " I would much rather live on dry bread and have my hands busy in the Lord's work than feast on luxuries and be idle."

There was one army officer who was so afraid of being converted that he ran away. His wife had become a Christian and invited people to her drawing-room to hear the Gospel so this man went off to one of his country estates and hid there for two months.

At the end of that time he thought to himself, " I will return to the city. These meetings must be over by now and I shall be quite safe." So back he came. When he reached his own house he met people on the doorstep, just going in to a service. Being a gentleman he felt obliged to be polite to them and he went in, too, though he was very much annoyed.

At that meeting he saw for the first time what Jesus had done for him. He said afterwards, " It was as if a ray from heaven shot through my heart. I ran into my bed-room and gave myself to God."

These wonderful things happened, day after day and month after month, not because an English Doctor went about giving talks on the Bible, but because the Holy Spirit of God was at work and was using this man and others as His instruments.

WITHIN PRISON WALLS

IF Dr. Baedeker loved to be of service to the Russian nobles there was another class of people whom he was still more eager to help. These were the poor prisoners in the gaols and the great fortresses, in the hard labour camps and the mines.

For the most part they were very cruelly treated. They had not even room to sleep properly at night and, in fact, scarcely enough air to breathe. The evil-smelling quarters in which they were kept used to remind him of the Black Hole of Calcutta. You have probably heard of that and you know how more than a hundred people died there in a single night, just for want of air.

The dirt and the smells and the insects caused sickness, and fever and small pox carried many off. One of the most deadly diseases is typhus and that was very common. Most people would be afraid to go and visit such dreadful places, but Dr. Baedeker had no fear for he was sure that God had sent him with a message to those poor sufferers, and He would take care of him.

In some prisons there were deep dungeons and men were shut up quite alone in their damp cells, and had to lie on the cold stone floor with the rats running over them in the dark.

Prisoners were made to march in gangs from one gaol to another or from Russia proper into far Siberia and chains were fastened to their legs which made it very painful to walk. It would have been hard enough to trudge those weary miles at best, but dragging a chain it was a great deal worse, and their poor ankles became terribly sore.

There was no one to take pity on them. If people saw them on the march they would merely think, " They are bad men and they are getting their punishment." Dr. Baedeker never felt like that : he was only very, very sorry.

He was rather like a certain Englishman named John Newton, some of whose hymns you may possibly find in your Church Hymn-book. One day he saw a prisoner being led away by a policeman and he said, "But for the grace of God, there goes John Newton." He meant that he might have been just as bad himself if God had not taught him otherwise.

Dr. Baedeker knew besides that the prisoners were not all bad men by a long way. Many of them were being unjustly punished and were separated from their homes and dear ones for no reason at all. He longed to speak some word of comfort to them or to do them some little kindness.

But the officials were so hard and the rules were so strict that there did not seem much chance of ever getting inside the frowning walls of those terrible prison fortresses. The Doctor could do nothing, but happily he knew that God could do everything. So he prayed and waited. One day he told a certain noble lady of his wish for a permit to visit the prisons. She was herself a friend of the Empress, but she did not think anything could be done and she sadly shook her head. When she went home, however, she told her husband, the Count, what the Doctor was wanting.

Some time afterwards this lady was shopping in St. Petersburg and the Count was patiently waiting at the door for her when suddenly he cried out, "Come here quickly!" She hurried to him, saying, "What's the matter?" "There is the very man you want, on the other side of the road." "Whom do you mean?" "The Director of the Prisons Department. He is the man to speak to, about the permit you have been wanting."

"Run, then," cried the Countess, "and call him back!" So the Count ran and brought the official gentleman to the shop door. "May I have the honour to oblige your ladyship?" he asked, bowing low. "Thank you," said the Countess, "I should like you to supply my friend, Dr. Baedeker, an Englishman, with a permit to visit the prisons and see prisoners, to give them Bibles and do them good."

"Does your friend think he can reform them?" asked the big man. It seemed to him a rather queer request. "He thinks God can," said the lady, "through His Word, the Gospel."

Then the thing that had appeared so unlikely, in fact, almost impossible, actually happened. The Director gave his permission. "Indeed, madam, what you say is true. I will certainly see that he has the permit he requires." So Dr. Baedeker's prayers were answered and God put it into the official's heart to give him what he needed.

That was a very big thing indeed. It said he was " under special command to visit the prisons of Russia and to supply the convicts with copies of the Holy Scriptures." It allowed him to go to every prison in the country, from Warsaw to the island of Saghalien. You can't understand what a vast territory this was unless you look at the map.

One day he lost his precious permit, but it was not his own fault. He had been spending the day with eight hundred convicts, all in chains, who were going to start on foot for Siberia in the morning. Staying too long to try and comfort them, he missed his train, and had to spend half the night at the railway station. When the next train came in a great crowd was waiting for it and in the scramble for seats his pocket-book was stolen. It contained not only his permit but also his passport, his ticket, a good deal of Russian money and a hundred pounds in English bank notes. Indeed, it was a big loss!

When he reached Moscow he sat down and wrote to his friend the Countess and told her all about it. She replied by this telegram, " I am getting another order for you. But have you lost anything else, any money?" When she heard, she and others made up everything that had been stolen, because they so truly sympathised with the work among the prisoners. The new permit was in some ways even better than the old one. So God made everything to work out for the best.

THE BEST OF GIFTS

YOU will remember that the Russian peasants had their own pet name for Dr. Baedeker and called him "Dedouchka," or "Dear Grandfather." He well deserved that title, and the sight of his kind face did many a sad heart good.

In one prison he saw a boy of thirteen and asked why he was there. His father had committed a murder and the lad knew of it but kept quiet. He would not tell on his own father, and who could blame him for this? The Russian law did blame him though, and condemned him to go to prison for two years. Here he not only suffered great hardship, but he began to grow as wicked as the men among whom he lived. When Dear Grandfather passed that way he pleaded for him and obtained his pardon, and in a little while he was able to take him back to his mother.

The prisoners felt the kindness of this good man's heart even before he spoke to them, and they always found him glad to do them any little service that he could. In one prison they told him they longed for a little tea. So he went to a tea-merchant and got him to make up packages of brick tea and sugar, one for each, and he took them round in the morning. He also got spectacles for some who could not read without them.

These kindnesses made the prisoners feel that somebody loved them after all: somebody cared. They were the more ready then to believe that God loved them and would listen if they prayed to Him. "God loves you! God loves you!" It was most wonderful news, and seemed too good to be true, yet something in their hearts told them that the Doctor was right. They learned to know the Saviour who endured for us far more terrible suffering than any one else has ever had to bear, and they were comforted. Not all of them, of course, but some here and some there.

Russian Prisoners on the road to Siberia

Wherever he went the Doctor carried large quantities of the Scriptures, chiefly New Testaments and Gospels. These he gave to the prisoners when he had made sure that they could read. The British and Foreign Bible Society supplied them to him and he distributed them carefully, for they were much too precious to waste. This society, by the way, has published the Scriptures in more than six hundred languages and sent them all over the world. We who cannot do big things for God can save our pennies to buy Gospels and there is no telling what may come of this.

In a certain prison not far from the Black Sea Dr. Baedeker and his interpreter talked to a large company of men of several nationalities and then gave each of them the present of a New Testament in his own language. They were marched up in rows to receive them and took them very gratefully. One of the warders said, " We have a murderer here now : he is down in the dungeon." The doctor begged to be taken to his cell and offered him a book like the rest. " I can't read," he said hopelessly.

Then the visitor took out of his pocket a strange little book, without a word of print in it. It had three leaves only : the first was black, the second red and the third white. " Whatever does this mean ? " asked the convict, " I don't understand."

" The black page stands for sin," said the Doctor, " your sin and mine. The red one is to tell you that the blood of Jesus Christ, God's Son, cleanseth us from all sin. If we put our trust in Him our hearts will be made white like this last page. Suppose you pray this short prayer : ' Wash me and I shall be whiter than snow.' "

The convict took the little book and his hand shook as he turned it over. " You can read that now, can't you ? " the Doctor asked gently. " Yes, I can read it, thank God ! " he replied, " and thank you, sir, a thousand times for bringing such a message to such a wretch as I am."

And thus this messenger of Christ went from prison to

prison bringing hope into the most desolate hearts. When he returned to the same places a year or two later the men told him what the Bible or the New Testament had meant to them and how they had learned to know the love of God. Some of them had made cardboard cases in which to keep this special treasure so that it might not get soiled or rubbed.

You must not think it was easy to do this work for the prisoners. Although when "Dedouchka" showed his permit no gaoler could refuse to let him in, the officials could make themselves very unpleasant sometimes. The police employed spies to watch him, and they followed him along the street and lounged about the door of his hotel. They even got into the servants' hall in those houses where he was entertained as a guest and anything that they could learn about him they reported to those higher up.

When Dear Grandfather was giving away Gospels he often marked in red ink the special texts which he thought would be helpful to the men. Sometimes he made a cross in the margin to call attention to them.

One day a high prison officer saw him giving out his Testaments and asked, "What are these red signs?" "I have only underlined some special texts," the Doctor said, "to help them to understand better." "We can't have this," cried the big man. "It is against the regulations. Warder, collect the books that have been given out: the men must not have them."

Dr. Baedeker was quite puzzled and said he did not know he had broken any rule. "The regulations say," continued the officer, "that you can give away Bibles or Testaments without note or comment. These lines and crosses mean something: they are your own notes and comments. Warder," he repeated, " Gather them up at once. The men can't have them."

Happily the Doctor had some more which had not been marked and he gave them these instead. But you see it was no easy task that he had in hand. Usually he won his way with those stern officials by his good temper and politeness and some of them became quite friendly and used to look forward to his visits.

THE TARANTASS

WHEN Baedeker was a boy, though he dreamed of travelling, he had no idea of the vast journeys he would some day make. Indeed, when we read about them now it is hard for ourselves to grasp the distances he covered. His permit said he might go all over Russia to visit the prisons, but how big is Russia?

The United States is a great country and of its forty-eight different states many are larger than England. It takes a week in an express train to get across from coast to coast, but this vast land is small compared with Russia.

Canada is even larger than the United States for it includes wide regions in the frozen north which are scarcely inhabited and little known, but it also is small compared with Russia.

India with its teeming millions of people, its great rivers and plains and its mighty mountains, is nevertheless smaller than either of these others. Russia is not only bigger than any of these, it is almost as big as all of them put together.*
As for our own little country, Russia would make nearly a hundred of it, at any rate, it is more than ninety-four times the size of Great Britain.

As you know, Russia is partly in Europe and partly in Asia and the Asiatic part is much the larger and is called Siberia. Here for more than two hundred years those who displeased the government have been sent to spend the rest of their days in hardship and misery. When in Moscow, " Dedouchka " sometimes saw great gangs of men, preparing to start on foot for that cruel land, to be shut up in its prisons and to slave in its mines.

As his heart was full of God's own love and pity he longed

*Not counting Alaska.

to go to every one of those places of punishment to carry a message of hope, and to tell the convicts that after this sad life there would be a happier one for those who put their trust in Jesus.

But it was no easy matter to reach those distant fortresses and camps. Nowadays there is a great railway which runs right across Siberia to the Pacific Coast and links up Moscow with the Far East. But in those days it was only just beginning to be built so " Dedouchka " had to get horses and drive from place to place. You will remember that in England before the railroad came people travelled by stage-coach and changed horses at the posting-stations. It was something like this with the Doctor, only instead of buying his ticket and taking his seat, he had to buy a carriage and hire horses from point to point.

The carriage was called a tarantass and it was something like an old-fashioned family coach. Its body was made of wicker-work lined with carpet and it had a movable leather hood. Alas! it had no springs so the jolting was dreadful. Three or four long poles on which the body rested did something to lessen the shocks but the going was rough at the best.

Of course they packed their belongings in such a way as to make themselves as comfortable as they could for those long journeys. First came a layer of books, perhaps five hundred Bibles and Testaments done up into parcels of forty each and well arranged in the bottom of the carriage as a sort of ballast. Then the rest of the luggage was put in and laid as level as possible. On top of all was spread a mattress and pillows for " Dedouchka " and his interpreter to use as a seat by day and a bed by night. Food for the trip had to be stowed away in the corner and they also carried boxes of grease for the wheels and some rope and a hatchet in case of a breakdown. For the way was so lonely that they could not be sure of getting help in difficulties.

Three horses were harnessed abreast to the tarantass and when all was ready off they went. The Siberian post-horses ran at great speed, the drivers urging them forward at a furious rate, but only by talking and shouting to them, not by the use of a whip. It was good to get over the ground so fast, but as the roads were very rough (sometimes, indeed, they were mere tracks), the travellers were pitched about in startling fashion and rolled from side to side, or knocked their heads against the ceiling. They had to hold on very tight to keep from being thrown out.

When they came to an inn they could get hot water and black bread and sometimes eggs. The water was heated in a samovar, a sort of urn with a central tube in which charcoal was burned. "Dedouchka" was very fond of black bread, but as he wanted more than that he had to carry it. They were obliged to do without butter but they would sometimes take a good-sized ham and hunger made the best sauce.

On one long journey their fare consisted of tea and eggs and dry bread in the morning, more bread and a quart of milk about two o'clock and tea and bread and sardines in the evening. They were then on their way to the city of Irkutsk, and when they arrived at ten o'clock at night, they quickly got a wash and sat down to a solid meal. The well-cooked cutlets, with the salad and potatoes tasted very good to them that time. They found the bed ever so comfy after rolling about in the tarantass on top of the luggage, and being waked up every little while by a rougher jolt than usual.

When the doctor had driven through Siberia, almost from end to end, and had reached the point where he could take a river steamer for the rest of the way, he sold the tarantass. He was quite sorry to part with it. Here is what he said about it in one of his letters home: "It seems hard to dispose of the dear old thing in such an unfeeling way, yet this is its lot. It has done us good service. Besides carrying us, it has been loaded with many hundreds of books. We have got attached to the conveyance in which we have been made to feel our bones very often, but in which also we have had much joy and comfort, much praise and prayer." To him it was more than a rickety Russian coach, it was something that had been used in the service of God to bring a message from heaven to some of the saddest places upon earth.

A PEEP INTO SIBERIA

WHILE I have told you about the carriage in which Dear Grandfather travelled, I have not yet told you about the country through which he went. Siberia is a land of great variety. It has high mountains on whose peaks the snow never melts, and broad barren marshes called " tundras," which are frozen the greater part of the year. There are also dense forests which have never been fully explored. Some of the longest rivers in the world are there and their tributaries are important waterways in themselves.

The crossing of rivers where there were no bridges formed one of " Dedouchka's " chief difficulties and sometimes he was in serious danger. Now and again he came across other travellers in trouble and was able to lend them a hand. One night his interpreter found a lady sitting beside a river, hoping that a ferry-boat might come and take her across. She had waited on the bank most of the night all alone. Her husband was an exile and she had followed him all the way from St. Petersburg, for it was her one desire to join him and share his hard lot. She was only twenty-seven, but her hair had turned perfectly white through her trouble. What a brave woman she was!

Siberia has many lakes of which the biggest is L. Baikal. It is the deepest lake in the world and there are only five larger ones. It is almost surrounded by mountains and their steep granite precipices come sheer down to the water-side and continue into the depths below. Steamers ply upon it carrying tea and grain, and when the Doctor reached the shore he was very pleased to see one there. It soon shipped tarantass and all and conveyed them safely to the other side.

Journeying still eastward he came to the great river Amoor, which flows between Russia and China. The scenery was grand and wild and the stream was full of fish, but he saw few men. The oak trees were very fine. Here and there he noticed oil oozing out of the rocks. Oil, of course, is very valuable and this was going to waste.

When " Dedouchka " could travel by river he was glad to do so, for it was not nearly so rough and rocky as driving by road. Also it was easier to manage his big load of books. On one steamer the captain was rather surly and asked, " What have you got in those cases ? " " Bibles and Testaments," was the reply.

" A likely story that," growled the captain. " Whatever do you mean to do with them ? " " Take them to the prisons," said the Doctor.

" Do you mean to sell them ? Convicts don't have much cash." " No, I mean to give them freely. Convicts have souls."

" Well, it seems rather queer to be giving goods away for nothing. I should like to have a look inside." " Open as many cases as you choose," said the Doctor quietly.

The captain called a sailor who stood near. " Here, . . . you ! Break open one of these cases and let us see what is inside." It was done, and though the captain dived down to the bottom and tumbled the contents out upon the deck he found nothing except what the Doctor had said, Bibles and Testaments. He tried another case with the same result.

" Put the books back," he said to the sailor, and turning to Dr. Baedeker he asked, " Who are you, sir ? " The Doctor gave him his name and address. " You come from England ? " " Yes." " And you've come to this country to give presents of Bibles to our Russian criminals?" "Yes." "You get a good salary, I imagine?" "None at all." "Who pays your expenses then?" "I do myself." "Well, well," exclaimed the captain, quite sorry for his rudeness, "I wish I might let you travel on this steamer free of charge, but at least you shall not pay a single kopek for the carriage of your boxes."

Sometimes "Dedouchka's" way lay through dense forests, utterly lonely, and almost dark. Only above the narrow strip of road did the light come through. Looking to right and left of it they could not see the sky, they could only see the tiny ribbon of blue just in front of them where the trees had been cut away. After being thus closed in for perhaps two days, they would emerge and find themselves on a broad plain where herds of horses and cattle were grazing.

Dear Grandfather loved the wild flowers and often wished he could take some home to Mrs. Baedeker and Emmie. Sometimes the hillsides were covered with them and the country seemed like one great garden in which were blended many lovely shades, such as blue, golden yellow, pale violet and pink. Peonies and other flowers that we cultivate here at home grew wild in great abundance, and better still, he sometimes saw the edelweiss, that little Alpine blossom that everybody loves.

There was one drawback in the midst of all this beauty and that was the presence of mosquitoes and gnats. Oh, what a nuisance they were! Mosquitoes, indeed, are worse than a nuisance, for some of them carry disease. People on the spot wore masks to protect themselves. These were made of something like horsehair, a large hood of it covering the head and shoulders. They gave the wearers a rather frightful appearance: they looked worse than scare-crows.

Although on his long journeys "Dedouchka" would travel hour after hour and meet very few people, when he reached the towns and cities that lay along the route, at once all was business and bustle. Men of many different nationalities jostled each other in the streets. Indeed, if I mentioned the languages they spoke you would say you had never heard of them. When you read of these people later on, remember that most of them have no knowledge of the Gospel, for the Christian nations that ought to have passed it on to them have sadly neglected to do so.

In this little-known part of the world there are interesting cities with shops full of gorgeous fabrics, and the merchants are sometimes enormously rich. Some of these shops are almost like exhibitions in themselves and they have different departments like our English stores, and are really five or six large businesses under one roof.

But after all, it was not the gay shops and the foreign manners and customs that interested Dear Grandfather, but the crowds of poor unhappy men in the prisons. If you will look at the picture you will see him standing on his cart talking to them. (The tarantass could not carry all the books so sometimes he took a cart as well.) Would you like to read in his own words about that day's work? He wrote: "Everything was arranged for us by the officers in charge, so we had open-air meetings of prisoners and proclaimed the Gospel to them freely and fully. In the evening 400 or 500 men returned from work. We had them drawn up in a square, and Kargel and I, standing on the cart on which our books were, spoke to them all, the officers also listening most attentively."

You can't imagine how glad some of those poor prisoners were to receive a Testament. Many tried to say how grateful they felt. Some wept for joy. Others fell on their faces on the ground and thanked God. In some of the prisons no Bibles had ever been given away before and no one had ever been to preach the Gospel there. To tell the Good News of salvation in a corner of the earth where it had never been heard was a wonderful joy to the Doctor. He felt as St. Paul used to feel. You remember the apostle was a great traveller and he said he loved to make Christ known, not where he was already named, but in the regions beyond. Perhaps even to you this privilege may one day be granted if you yield your life to God while you are young and let Him make what He will of it.

BRAVE WITNESSES

THE prisoners and exiles to whom Dear Grandfather tried to carry comfort were not all bad people by any means. Some of them were splendid Christians who were being persecuted for their loyalty to Christ. You have already seen from the story of Colonel Paschkoff that the Czar drove some of his best subjects out of the country because they did not worship God in just the same way as he did himself.

In Russia the way of the Greek Church was considered the right or " orthodox " way, and those who belonged to other denominations, such as the Baptists and the Quakers, were looked upon as heretics. There were many others besides these who tried to worship and serve God according to the teaching of the Bible. They said they needed no priest to grant them the forgiveness of their sins for they could come direct to the Heavenly Father in the name of Jesus. Their neighbours bowed down to the icons, or sacred pictures, but they saw no use in these, neither did they seek the help of the saints, who after all, had been sinners just like themselves.

They met together to study the Word of God and they were very happy people because they had given up the attempt to save themselves by their own good works and were trusting in what Jesus did for us upon the Cross. Their numbers grew rapidly and this greatly angered the Czar. He said, " I would rather be king of a desolate land than rule over a nation of heretics."

He employed one very cruel man to deal with these people,

A Russian Cottagers' House showing Icon in the corner.

and for about thirty years the truest Christians in Russia were treated like criminals. They were fined large sums of money, their houses and lands were taken away, they were sent to prison or driven into exile.

In the *Penal Code*, or book of punishments, we may read what wicked rules were enforced against them. For leaving the Orthodox Church to join another, the penalty was transportation or, " in milder cases eighteen months in a reformatory." For preaching or writing books about the truth they believed, they could be imprisoned in a fortress for as much as four years. For " spreading the views of heretics or aiding such " the punishment was exile to Siberia or some other distant part of the Empire.

Dr. Baedeker often met these brave witnesses for Christ, as he travelled from place to place. Being an Englishman himself, and having powerful friends at Court, he was able to be of service to them. Sometimes he contrived to meet them in the dead of night, in lonely places and took them gifts and loving messages from their fellow Christians in Great Britain.

Now and again in visiting the prisons he came across a party of these faithful people, on their way to exile. He was warned by the officials not to have much to do with them, but at least he could give them a hand-shake and a word of cheer. In one place he found seven fine Christian men with their families, twenty-seven all told, banished for their faith. A grandmother was among them and she said that this was the eleventh prison in which she had stayed on the way.

When the cruel government had marched such people out of Russia proper into the wilds of Siberia they let them go " free " and they might pick up a living as best they could. Often it was almost impossible to get enough to eat. And all the time the police were ordered to keep a sharp look-out on them.

If you read the New Testament carefully you will see that the Lord Jesus told His disciples beforehand that those who were true to Him would have to suffer persecution. The apostles also said that Christians must not think it strange if they had fiery trials to bear. But the Lord never fails His people at such times and always gives them strength and courage sufficient for the day.

The Doctor was once visiting a village to which some Christians had been banished. It was hidden among the mountains and the journey thither was very dangerous, for the road ran along the edge of a steep precipice. Worse still, robbers might at any moment be crouching among the rocks. But Dear Grandfather was glad to go to take a little cheer to those friends in trouble, and they were overjoyed at the sight of him. Writing home he said, " They meet in each other's rooms and sing and pray together." So you see if people only have Jesus with them, they can feel like singing anywhere !

NOAH'S COUNTRY

DR. BAEDEKER'S work took him to many lands besides Siberia. In one of his most interesting journeys he crossed the Caucasus Mountains and travelled over the region that lies between the Black and Caspian Seas. If you will take a look at the map you will see that here Russia, Persia and Turkey meet.

He saw Mount Ararat, where the ark rested after the Flood rising snow-capped above the plain. He visited Baku, a very queer sort of place. It is the city of oil wells and here, instead of trees, was a forest of pumping engines. Even the grass found it hard to grow, and the air, like the soil, was full of the smell of naphtha.

Now and then the Doctor met a caravan of Tartars coming down from the mountains to spend the winter in the plain. They had their droves of cattle, horses and sheep. The children rode donkeys and the fowls had sense enough to stick on the backs of the cows. It made " Dedouchka " think of the stories in the Bible about Abraham, Isaac and

Jacob, who used to wander from place to place with all their possessions.

These journeys were not without danger. The high mountain passes were difficult to cross and robbers lurked among the rocks. But Dr. Baedeker felt it was well worth while if he could take the Gospel to some village which seldom heard it, or meet a company of Armenian Christians who badly needed comfort. You have probably heard that the Armenians have long been cruelly persecuted by the Turks on account of their faith and thousands of them have been done to death.

There are various wild animals in those mountain districts, such as wolves and leopards and boars, but the doctor did not happen to come across them. A far more real danger was the soft harmless-looking snow which, like a white blanket, covered everything in an hour or two and made the travellers lose their way.

One Christmas " Dedouchka " visited a certain mountain village which was difficult to reach. The people had invited him several times before and he had never been able to go, so now, although it was rather risky, he felt he ought to try. When he left, with his guide, a party of Christians went some distance with him, but at last said good-bye and returned to their homes. The two tramped on, hour after hour, and towards evening the guide began to look uneasy. Night falls suddenly in those parts and he knew that in a few minutes it would be dark. He stood still and gazed around and then confessed to the doctor that he had lost his way.

" Is there nothing you can recognise ? " asked Dear Grandfather. " Nothing to show us our whereabouts, or the direction we should take ? " " I have been searching in vain for some sign," he replied. " Alas ! we shall both be dead of cold before morning."

" Then, let us just kneel down where we are and tell our Heavenly Father about it."

"Oh dear, oh dear, I wish I had not been so foolish as to venture on such a journey at such a time," cried the Armenian.

"God can take care of us and direct us. We will pray about it," urged the doctor.

"Most likely we are many hours' journey from a human habitation," the guide went on, "and as for me, I can't walk any farther. I shall never see my home again."

"Come, come, stop lamenting and pray. If you don't know the way, God does."

So they knelt down and the Doctor said: "Father, we cannot be lost for we are in Thy hand all the time and under the shadow of Thy wing. Thou knowest the way that we take. Send us help in our need and guide us to safety."

The prayer was interrupted by the distant barking of a dog. "Listen, that is our Father's answer. He has not kept us waiting," said the Doctor. They turned in the direction of the sound and it led them to a small Tartar encampment. The Tartars were very surprised to see them and thought it was a great wonder they had escaped death.

Dr. Baedeker told them how God answers prayer and they listened attentively as he went on to give them the story of the Gospel. They treated the travellers very kindly and Dear Grandfather and his Armenian friend greatly enjoyed their supper that Christmas night, though it was only a chunk of black bread and a pomegranate apiece.

GOODBYE, GRANDFATHER!

NOW, after taking these long journeys with Dr. Baedeker, sharing in imagination his tarantass and boat and sleigh, we shall have to say good-bye to him. Look once again at his picture. What a loving face he has! We don't wonder that the peasants called him "Dear

Russian Soldiers and Village Priest.

Grandfather." People sometimes said he made them think of the Apostle John, the one who wrote so much about the love of God, and whose own heart was so full of it.

Recalling now what we know of his life we see he was sent as a messenger to the very highest and the very lowest, to the princes and nobles in Russia's grandest society and to the prisoners in the dungeon. For though prince and prisoner may seem very far apart, they both alike need a Saviour. The Bible says, " There is no difference for all have sinned."

You and I are included in that " ALL." But happily we are included in another ALL as well : " All we like sheep have gone astray, we have turned every one to his own way, and the Lord hath laid on Him the iniquity of us ALL."

If we know that Jesus has borne our sins upon the Cross and we are " ransomed, healed, restored, forgiven," as the hymn says, then we shall want every one to share this happiness. We shall do everything we possibly can to spread the Good News to the ends of the earth.

HORACE UNDERWOOD OF KOREA

THE HERMIT LAND

> If you meet a foreigner
> **KILL HIM.**
> Whoever is friendly with him
> is a traitor to his country.

NOT much more than fifty years ago this notice might be seen posted on the highways of Korea. The people of this little country believed in keeping themselves to themselves. They wanted nothing to do with the rest of the world. They had been most cruelly treated by a powerful enemy three hundred years before, and now they asked to be left alone, and threatened trespassers with death.

So their country became known as the Hermit Land. You have heard how hermits used to live in the desert, all by themselves in some cave or hut, speaking to nobody, and quite content to be as poor as church mice. Korea deserved this nick-name up to half a century ago.

But where *is* Korea? Could you point it out on the map, without looking in the index? As our story concerns a man who went there, we had better be quite clear about it. Our first tale was about Siberia, the vast country whose name is sprawled right across the north of Asia. It takes no hunting to find that. Now if you will put your finger anywhere on the east coast of Siberia and draw it downwards, you will come to Korea. Just for a very few miles this little country borders on the big one; the dwarf touches the hand of the giant. But after all, though it is so tiny compared with Siberia (or Asiatic Russia), it is about the same size as our own land.

It was because of its big neighbours, Russia, China and Japan that Korea was so nervous of foreigners. When single ones came, the natives thought they were spies. It was, of course, very wrong and foolish to wish to kill them, but the idea was that if the Koreans did not do so, they might get killed themselves or at least be robbed of their liberty. Their fears were not without reason and since the days when that notice was put up, Korea has been conquered by Japan, and now it forms a part of the Japanese Empire. But at the time when our story begins it was still a free country with its own king.

Its history goes back a very long way for its first king began to reign about the same time as Saul, the first king of Israel, some eleven hundred years before Christ. His name was Kija and they say he came down from China with part of an army which had been defeated in battle. Korea was then inhabited by wild tribes who knew nothing of settled government. They soon saw that this stranger was far wiser than themselves so they made him king and he reigned over them for forty years.

He gave them good laws and introduced Chinese books and various customs that were better than their own. His memory has been honoured ever since. I have visited his grave and can tell you that after these three thousand years it is still kept neat and tidy.

When we speak of " books " of course we don't mean printed ones such as we have to-day. In those old times they were written by hand and there were not many copies of each. But the Koreans, like the Chinese, learned the secret of printing by the use of movable letters, long before this idea dawned on the people of the West.

It is said that they put up the first suspension bridge ever built in the world, all in a hurry on a summer's day, to meet a sudden need. The foe had invaded their land,

and in order to drive him back the king and his army had to cross a certain river. There was not any bridge and it was much too difficult for swimming or wading.

A quick-witted captain sent his men into the woods to get wistaria. Yes, you may well open your eyes and ask what was the good of that. Slight as it looks, its strands are wonderfully strong and the soldiers bound them together, threw them across the stream and fastened the ends to trees on either bank. Then they tightened up the slack cables by twisting them with sticks and a batch of men quickly laid down cross-pieces of wood and covered them with sod. So they soon had a bridge for the use of the king and his army.

You would think that a nation which showed itself so clever in its youth would go on making inventions and outstrip its neighbours in arts and manufactures. But no, it came to a stand-still, as did its big brother, China.

When Europeans gained permission to enter the Hermit Land, half a century ago, they felt as if they had dropped back into the Middle Ages. They found no factories but it was surprising to see what beautiful work the people were doing in their little mud houses. There were no saw-mills: two men would pull a long, narrow saw between them and so cut up a log.

The carpenter and the cabinet-maker, with very poor tools, turned out handsome chests, which formed the chief furniture of the home. These were trimmed with brass and sometimes inlaid with mother-of-pearl. The foreign visitors found beautiful brass-work, and indeed those who go there to-day often long to carry a trunkful home, but it is made not in great work-shops, but in little shacks built of mud and thatched with straw. It is the same with pottery. You can visit the potter's house and see him moulding the jars and bowls on his wheel and trimming them afterwards with his knife.

So while other countries were making all sorts of comforts

and conveniences by means of machinery, Korea remained where she was in the days of long ago, content to have a very few things, and these made at home by hand. This came of being a Hermit and not wishing to mingle with other nations. Less than fifty years ago, a foreigner happened to meet the governor of a certain Korean province, an important person, of course, and supposed to be educated. But as they talked, this gentleman was obliged to confess that he had never heard of England or America and he thought that the West was all one country.

A great change has taken place in recent times and nowadays Koreans are eager to know all about the rest of the world and to have their share in the improvements that science has brought about. Better still, they have welcomed the Gospel. A few years ago, at a great Christian conference, it was agreed that the best speech of all was made by a Korean.

HORACE AT SCHOOL

ALL this time that I have been telling about Korea, you have been waiting to be introduced to Horace Underwood, whose name is at the head of the story. Too bad! But you shall wait no longer.

Horace was a British boy, born in London, Number Four out of half a dozen children. His father was a chemist, not merely making up medicines and selling them but manufacturing his own drugs. He was, in fact, a scientist, always on the watch for new ideas, and quick to find a use for them. He invented a special kind of ink and he improved type-writer ribbons.

No doubt you have heard of the Underwood type-writer. Perhaps your father has one in his office, and though maybe he uses a Remington or a Royal or some other make, still you may be sure there is an Underwood not far away. It was Horace's brother John who became a manufacturer and sent his type-writers all over the world. John and Horace were the best of friends.

But we are going much too fast. Let us turn back and begin again. The Underwood children had a very happy home and a wonderful mother. No one ever saw her angry or heard her speak an unkind word. All the week their father was busy in his factory but he spent Sunday afternoons with them, after they got back from the Mission School, and they loved those times with him.

But troubles came as troubles will. They lost their dear mother and their baby sister and home never seemed the same again. Then their father was cheated by his partner and instead of enjoying the success he deserved, he found his business was beginning to fail.

About this time Horace and his brother Fred were sent to a boarding-school in France, by the seaside. They slept in a big dormitory where most of the boys were French but a few were English. As usual, when they were ready for bed, they knelt down to say their prayers. At this the other fellows began yelling like wild animals but the Underwoods paid no attention. Then there followed a rain of pillows, boots and hair-brushes, in fact all sorts of things that happened to be handy. Fred and Horace finished their prayers and climbed into bed. For several nights this went on. At last the other British boys began to feel they must back up their own countrymen, so they knelt down too. By degrees the French boys followed their example and the dormitory got into the habit of saying its prayers.

One day Fred and Horace had a letter from home containing a great piece of news. Their father had made up his mind to go to America. Through his partner's dishonesty his business was in such a bad way that he thought he had better begin over again in a new country.

So he went, though sorry enough to leave old England, and the boys followed him.

It was not easy to start afresh, but Mr. Underwood was a brave and able man and little by little he made his way. The boys worked well in the ink factory and the garden, and their sister looked after the house. They all took a stand for Christ by joining the church as soon as they were settled in the new place.

Although they needed to work very hard to make both ends meet, their father felt he could not put Horace into business, as he had always wanted to be a missionary. So he sent him to school to be prepared for College. In America, lads with very little money are able to get a University education if only they work hard enough. The Underwoods were fond of quoting this line : " Faith laughs at impossibilities and says it shall be done ! " Isn't that a splendid way to treat difficulties? Instead of moping or grumbling or despairing, just to laugh ! People can do that if they are sure God is going to help them through.

So Horace Underwood became a student at New York University. His home was seven miles from the city and he could not afford to pay the fare, so he walked every day there and back and carried a light lunch in his satchel. It meant getting up at five o'clock in the morning and studying until twelve o'clock at night. I should not advise you to copy him in this. If he had not been extra strong he could not have kept it up for four years as he did. He took his degree at the University and then went on to a Theological College to be trained as a minister.

In the summer holidays he used to earn a little money to help him through the next term. One year he tried book-selling and went from house to house in country districts, carrying his pack. He was very successful and not only made good profits but some good friends besides. So by pluck and perseverance he won through and got the education that he needed to prepare him for his life-work.

He always thought he was going to India, but God had another sphere for him. In our next story we shall read how Arthur Neve expected to go to Africa but instead of that he was sent to Kashmir. Both alike had but one wish and aim, to obey their Lord and Master, so they gladly gave up their own ideas when they found out His Will.

EASTWARD HO!

WHEN Horace Underwood was in college, the students had a missionary meeting one day among themselves and one of them read a paper about the Hermit Land. A treaty had now been signed by which foreigners were to be allowed to live there. But though more than a year had passed no one had gone to make known the Gospel to its twelve millions of people.

Young Underwood was very much stirred up about this and he went out from the meeting to try and get recruits for Korea, or at any rate to persuade one man to go there. He himself was going to India, he said, and had already begun to prepare for his task. But he could not find anybody for Korea and at last he began to think that God meant him to change his plans and be His messenger to this needy country. So he asked the American Presbyterian Church to send him there and they did so.

Of course he had to finish his college course and before he was ready to sail a doctor had volunteered for Korea and he and his wife became the first Protestant missionaries there. They were Dr. and Mrs. Allen. Mr. Underwood followed them a year after. This was scarcely half a century ago, and now there are thousands upon thousands of Christians in Korea and it would be hard to find people in any country more eager to spread the Good News among their neighbours.

The doctor was called to attend a very important man, who was dangerously ill. He was something like a Prime Minister and was a cousin of the Queen. Under the blessing of God, Dr. Allen was able to save his life and the King and Queen at once became the warm friends of the missionaries. There was no Mrs. Underwood then, but she came a few years later, and as she was a lady doctor, she was made physician to the Queen. So we see that medicine has all along had a great deal to do with carrying the Gospel into Korea.

No doubt you want to know what sort of a country this was, and is. Mr. Underwood, too, used to wonder what it would be like, as he walked up and down the deck of the steamer on his way out to Japan. For he had to go there first and then take a little boat across the straits to Korea. At first sight the country looked very bleak and barren and along the coast were rocky islands on which next to nothing grew.

But once he got inland he found it very different, indeed, quite beautiful in many parts. Everywhere it is hilly and there is a proverb which says, "Over the mountains, mountains still, mountains without number." They are not bare, but green and fertile and often wooded and the valleys are covered with crops. There are no big rivers because there is no room for them, the mountains being so near the sea, but there are many little ones. The flowers are beautiful: those which we grow here in gardens and greenhouses are found wild there upon the mountain sides. How you would love to have a picnic and fill your baskets with roses and lilies of the valley, heliotrope and clematis and pink and white azaleas!

But the missionaries did not go to live in the country among the birds and flowers, though they could enjoy a little rest there now and then. They went to live among the people because they had a Message for them. It was at Seoul, the capital, that Mr. Underwood and his friends settled down. You pronounce this name just like "soul," your inner self, or "sole" the fish.

It was a very dirty place, so muddy in the rainy season that it was difficult to get through the streets at all. There were no covered drains, only open ditches by the roadside. There must have been millions of germs floating about ready to pounce on people!

In spite of all, however, Seoul was beautiful. Hundreds of years ago a great stone wall was built to protect it which, though now broken, is still a fine monument. It wound up and down over the mountains. No one could help admiring the splendid view and Mr. and Mrs. Underwood and the other missionaries soon came to love their adopted home.

But they cared for the people much more than the place, and I am sure they loved the boys and girls best of all. Korean children are very much like English ones; they play when they can, and work when they must. Sometimes they do both together. Very small people often have to carry a baby brother or sister tied on to their backs. I have seen them playing hop-scotch in the streets and jumping from square to square, while poor baby's head was bobbing up and down. The boys are fond of flying kites and these are much prettier than ours and made in all sorts of wonderful shapes. Girls enjoy the see-saw which tosses them high into the air like bouncing balls.

For boys who had no parents or friends the missionaries opened an orphanage. Once Mr. Underwood found a wee chappie of four, dying for lack of proper food and so hungry that he was trying to eat the paper off the walls. He took him home, and although he was a bachelor in those days, he cared for this baby until he became well and strong. You may have heard of "Tiny Tim": this was Tiny Kim. He turned out to be a clever lad and he easily learned English along with his mother tongue. When he grew up he became Mr. Underwood's private secretary and better still, he was a true Christian.

A COSY HOME

NOT many of our English homes have central heating, but the Koreans have it in their little mud houses and it does not cost much, either. The floor is made of flat stones, not close together, but so laid that there are narrow passages, or flues, between them. Just outside the house, at the end of one of these flues, is the fire. The heat passes from it, through the flues, and out at the farther side of the living-room, into a hole which serves as a chimney.

The stone floor is covered with a special sort of mud and over it is laid brown oiled paper which looks like polished wood. On this the Koreans spread their neat matting and they all sit cross-legged on it and keep their toes warm.

The children help to make home comfortable for they go into the woods and gather sticks for the fire. If these are not plentiful they get dry grass and weeds from the roadside or fill up their baskets with dead leaves.

Once I watched some men building a house. After they had put up strong posts to bear the roof they propped these with smaller pieces of wood and then between them they wove a sort of basket work. Next they plastered this over with mud to make the walls and added a coat of white-wash. With the straw of their own rice-fields the Koreans make a thick thatch for the roof and when all is done the home is very cosy and warm.

So long as it does not rain too hard ! Rain is bad for mud ! Dry mud can be quite comfortable but wet mud is a mess. One night during a heavy storm the missionaries had to spread mackintoshes over their beds and put up their umbrellas. Although they were in such a sorry plight, they could not help laughing at the funny picture they made. Mr. Underwood was one of the people whose faces get broad instead of long at such times.

I wonder how you would like to have dinner in a Korean house. You would need to practise using chop-sticks first, or you would go hungry while the rest were eating whole bowlsful of rice. I can't tell you just what you would get, for that would depend on whether the friends were well-to-do or poor, and whether it was a feast or an ordinary meal. Very likely there would be kuksu, a nice dish of vermicelli with bits of meat, swimming in soup. You would not care for the bread, I am afraid; it is too much like india rubber.

The Koreans themselves think nothing can beat kimchi. This is a sort of pickle and they eat it all the year round, for every meal. Kimchi at breakfast, kimchi at dinner, kimchi at supper; they never seem to tire of it. In the autumn the women make a big supply, put it up in jars, and leave it to ferment, if you know what that means. You would soon understand if you lived there, for it would gradually begin to smell. When it smells nearly strong enough to knock you down, then it is perfect and ready to eat.

Ever so many things go to the making of it, so it would puzzle any one to say what it tastes of in the end. The chief ingredients are cabbage and turnips and red peppers. There are also bits of fish, and the housewife will most likely add oil and ginger and garlic, which accounts for part of the smell. A wonderful hodge podge it is, and no mistake!

One of the trials of missionaries is eating things they don't like. If you are finicky about your food, don't talk about being a missionary when you grow up. Once when Mr. Underwood was taking a country trip he stopped at a certain village, and as he sat in the guest-room, in the evening, a farmer came in with a beaming face and said he had brought a present for the pastor. He reached far up into the sleeve of his dirty garment and brought out a pancake in which were wrapped some cold potatoes. Everybody thought this was a great treat and they all stood around to see the missionary enjoy it. Poor Mr. Underwood! Can you guess how he felt? Many people would have made some excuse and declined it but he thanked his farmer friend and ate it up then and there. Do you know why? The apostle Paul once said we should be ready to bear anything rather than " hinder the Gospel of Christ " and the missionary felt the poor farmer might be offended, and so hindered in believing on Jesus, if he refused that cold pancake out of his dirty sleeve.

Talking of sleeves reminds me that I have not told you how the Koreans dress. The men wear a long white garment, with streamers fastened in a bow on the left side, and round their heads they have a tight band of horse-hair with an odd little hat perched upon it. The hair is tied in a knot which stands straight up like a short stalk, so the Koreans are sometimes called the Top-Knots. Women and girls have full short skirts and tight bodices. But the fashions are changing very fast. Many have now cut off their top-knots and put on Western clothes. Some are half East and half West which is rather funny. School-boys and school-girls wear neat uniforms and before long the people of the former " Hermit Land " will be dressing much as we do here.

MR. NO SAYS " YES "

ONE evening in an inland city, Mr. Underwood and another missionary sat talking. Suddenly they were startled by a cry of " Fire," and they jumped up and hurried to the spot to see if they could help. The fire had not made much headway and a well was close at hand, so it was plain that a few energetic men could soon put out the flames. But, strange to say, they were not even trying to do so.

Policemen were making a hullabaloo with trumpets and

Dr. Baedeker in Russia.

Series Six

Plate Tw

Dr. Underwood of Korea.

Dr. Arthur Neve of Kashmir.

horns and the owner and his family were weeping and wailing in front of the burning house. But tears, however fast they may flow, will not put out a fire, so the two missionaries seized buckets, filled them at the well and went to work. Before very long the flames were out and the house was saved.

You would expect the people to be grateful for this help. Not a bit of it! No one even said " Thank you," but angry whisperings were heard on all sides and some even talked of killing them. " The Fire God will be offended," they said. " To-night he will come and wreak vengeance on our town and likely enough many houses will be burnt down, because these foreigners have interfered."

Fortunately no other house took fire in the town that night; but in a country place five miles up the river one was burned to the ground, which of course might happen anywhere, at any time. Nevertheless, the poor, ignorant folk blamed the foreigners for this, and came into the town to punish them, but by that time they had slipped away.

The Fire God is only one of the crowd of deities and demons in whom the Koreans believe. The woods are full of them; every mountain and river, even every path and every house has its own special god. While some are reckoned fairly harmless, most of them are thought to be the enemies of men rather than their friends, and as for a god loving human beings and caring to make them happy, that is an unheard of idea.

The best way to do with the many gods and demons, the Koreans think, is to offer them sacrifices of food and beg them to leave one alone. If a child is very ill, mother will tear a little piece off its coat or dress, and go to visit a sacred tree. She carries on her head a gift of fruit or rice or wine and places it on the ground. Then she ties the rag upon one of the branches, praying that the spirit of disease may go into the cloth and leave her little one in peace.

Just think what Good News it was to the people of Korea to be told that God is Love, and that the Lord Jesus is stronger than all demons and spirits, so there is no need to be afraid of them, even if they are real. Most of them, of course, are not, any more than fairies and gnomes.

Perhaps you would like to hear about the first man who believed the News these missionaries brought and became a Christian. He had the shortest, easiest name you could possibly think of : Mr. No. But I don't think it fitted him very well for he was the first one to say " Yes " to the Gospel invitation.

Mr. No said " Yes " as soon as he understood, but it was some time before he did. He came across a book that described the lands of the West, and said their people were powerful and progressive (that is, go-ahead), but they professed the Christian faith, which was a very bad religion. I can't attempt to tell you the dreadful things this book said about Christianity. Mr. No, however, had a mind of his own and he thought to himself, " How is it that these nations have made such wonderful progress if they are founded on a wicked religion ? I can't quite believe it ; I must enquire further."

For several reasons he did not want anybody to know he was interested in the foreign religion. He dared not go to a Christian service or ask any plain questions. Now the two missionaries, Dr. Allen and Mr. Underwood, guessed there might be some men who would not come to church, but might be willing to meet them elsewhere. So they fitted up a " guest-room " in the Korean style and started a class for the study of English. Mr. No joined it, though English was not what he was after.

One day he was alone in the doctor's study for a few moments and he spied on his desk two little books, in Chinese, named " Matthew's Good News " and " Luke's Good News." Like many Koreans, Mr. No understood Chinese and in a jiffy he popped them up his sleeve. Sleeves are handy, you see. They will hold books and pancakes and many other things!

When he got home he went into his inner room and sat down to read. It was all so wonderful that, once he had begun, he could not stop till he had read both books through. In fact, he read and pondered over them all night long.

Early in the morning he went over to Mr. Underwood's house and confessed how he had taken the doctor's books off his desk. Mr. Underwood told him not to worry a bit about that, for Dr. Allen would be more than glad to let him have them.

"It's good! It's grand!" cried Mr. No, holding up the precious books. He was not afraid now; he was so full of the Good News that he was eager to talk about it. Do you remember the story of a man named Nathanael? The very first time that he saw Jesus he believed on Him and exclaimed, "Master, Thou art the Son of God: Thou art the King of Israel!" Mr. No was that sort of a man.

In that never-to-be-forgotten night, reading the wonderful story of the Gospel, he saw that this was not a mere "foreigners' religion," after all, but was the Good News of a Saviour who had died for the sins of the whole world.

So he confessed his new faith and was baptized, and little by little tens of thousands of Koreans followed his example. He must often have been glad that he did not hang back through fear of what people might say or do, but became Number One in that great company.

"PASS IT ON"

THE Good News spread throughout Korea in a most wonderful way. This was chiefly because the people themselves passed it on; when they heard it in the market or the street they went home and talked about it. They told their friends and neighbours that

God so loved the world that He gave His only-begotten Son to die for our sins upon the Cross. No one had ever dreamed of such love before. That all sins could be forgiven, at once, because Jesus had suffered in our stead, this was most amazing news.

Some people did not see a missionary at all, or hear one preach, but only met somebody who had seen one and who tried to pass the message on. They did not always understand it, and sometimes it was twisted in the telling, and sometimes they only got a bit of it and had to wait a long time for the rest.

A certain woman of We Ju went one day to visit friends in another town. While she was there she heard someone speak of the " Jesus doctrine." This was quite new to her; nobody knew anything about it where she came from. It was not much that her friends knew, either, but one of the neighbours had been on business somewhere else, and there he had heard Mr. Underwood tell the story of the Gospel. So he told his friends what he could remember and one of them told this visitor, and when she got back home she told her neighbours. But she could not tell them much because that man had not remembered a great deal.

You and I have our Bibles and we can read them every day so we don't need to depend on hearsay. But this woman had no Bible or Testament, nor even a Gospel. All she knew was this: There is only one God and we must worship no other. We must put away our sins and try to be good. We must keep one day in seven holy. We must sing, " Yesu We Patkui Umnay" (" Nothing but the blood of Jesus ").

Her great friend, when she heard this, thought it was very good, so they agreed together that, no matter what others did, they would worship the one true God. They would no longer pray to the spirits and demons in the woods and fields and streams. They tried to sing, " Nothing but the blood of Jesus," but they did not understand what it meant. Every seventh day they gave up to worship God as best they knew.

After a time a few others joined them. One of these was a very wicked man and a prize-fighter, but he wanted to be different. The woman herself kept a wine-shop and of course all sorts of people dropped in there and she shared what she knew with them.

At last one day a man came along with a pack on his back and books to sell. The books were New Testaments and Gospels and he spoke about the Lord Jesus. The two women and their friends were delighted to meet someone who could tell them more about Him and could explain the song which they had never understood. This colporteur, as the Bible-sellers are called, told them the whole story of the Gospel and how the Lord Jesus had died on Calvary to put away our sins. He also spoke to many others who gathered round and some of them came to believe.

But he said he was sorry to see that the worshippers of the true God were meeting in a wine-shop, for wine does so much harm, and the habit of drinking is likely to drive people away from God. Anybody can see that the poor drunkard has wandered away from Him, and if we offer people wine, or sell it to them, or even drink along with them, we shall be giving them a push in the wrong direction.

When the woman heard this she was very sorry she had been selling wine all those years, and she said at once that she would do so no longer. So out it all went into the ditch and the colporteur helped her to pour it away. She had to find something else to do for a living, but she did not wait to think about that. As soon as she saw what was right she did it. And of course God took care of her and did not let her come to want.

After a while these Christians built themselves a church and the people crowded in to hear God's Word. The number of believers kept on growing until there were seven hundred names on the roll. So then they had to enlarge their place of worship. As for that prize-fighter he became a true Christian and at last he was found worthy to be a preacher of the Gospel. So that is how the Good News spread in the place called We Ju.

HIKING

TO-DAY, railways run the whole length of Korea and there are fine motor roads, but forty years ago travelling was very slow. Mr. Underwood was the first foreigner to pass through the country and he made the trip partly on horseback and partly on foot. It was very dangerous in those days, and he went at the risk of his life. People had not forgotten that old notice, " If you meet a foreigner, kill him." True, it had been taken down from the roadside; but the countryfolk who had been taught all their lives to fear and hate the stranger, could not suddenly begin to love and trust him. This took time. But God watched over His servants and no harm came to them.

They would start early in the morning and travel on till noon, then stop at an inn, get some dinner, and preach to the crowd that gathered to gaze at them. On they would go again, travel till sunset and then put up for the night in another place. No doubt you think it would be " topping " to be out on the road from dawn till dark and see so much of a strange new land, and so it was at first. But it was tiring too, for after the long day's journey the main work had still to be done.

Mr. Underwood's task was to give the people the Gospel, but first he had to get the packs unloaded and his party settled in for the night. Then he brought out his books and old and young crowded around to look and buy. After supper he sat down in the men's room and talked with them by the hour, answering their questions and telling them about his Master. Or perhaps he had an open-air meeting by moonlight under some big stone gate or other spot where the people were used to gathering.

The missionaries generally carried food with them in their loads, as they never knew what sort of inns they would find. They might be decent or they might be very bad. Once Mr. Underwood and a doctor went off together on a long trip. It was not Dr. Allen this time, but Dr. Avison, who founded the splendid hospital for which Seoul is now famous.

The two men had some pleasant surprises and found the inns much better than they had expected. They wrote to their wives saying that the native food was very good. Whenever they met travellers going towards Seoul they asked them to carry these letters back.

Further along the way the two missionaries were expecting to find a parcel from home. Before they reached that distant point the inns had changed for the worse, the food was not nearly so good, and they were getting heartily tired of kimchi and kuksu and the bread that is like india rubber. They cheered each other up by imagining what that parcel would contain. Home-made bread ! A good big pie ! " I know what *my* wife will send" said Mr. Underwood. " And *I* know what *my* wife will send," replied the doctor.

So each boasted of his own wife and her splendid cooking, until at last they arrived at their destination, tired and hungry, and saw the parcel there, waiting for them. No, two parcels, beside a package of letters. Eagerly they opened parcel number one and the next moment it went flying across the room. Why ? Because there was nothing in it but a big india-rubber boot ! They tore open the other, and behold ! there was another boot ! It quickly followed its fellow to the far corner. Those two good men did not know whether to laugh or feel disgusted at first, but in a few minutes they got over their disappointment and enjoyed this joke against themselves. It was too funny after all their dreams of cake and pie! You see what it meant? After those early letters reached home, saying how they liked the Korean food, the two wives thought it was no use to send them any other. But Mrs. Avison, anxious lest her husband should take cold, tramping in the wet, thought he ought to have his long rubber boots. The two missionaries never ceased teasing their wives about the nasty, indigestible stuff they sent them when they were longing for a good meal and looking forward to that tuck-box straight from home.

There were many risks and dangers on these country trips. Sometimes Mr. Underwood had to wade through rivers which were swollen by the rains, and in which the current was so strong that he could scarcely hold his own. Then, after scrambling out, he had to travel on, drenched to the skin. Of course he had other clothes in his luggage, but as this was likely to be soaked through at the same time, they did him no good. Worse than flooded rivers were the roving bands of robbers, wandering about on dark nights in search of prey. In the mountains he heard of tigers and black bears, but I don't think he met any of them, though once a leopard ran right across his path.

One night Mr. and Mrs. Underwood were staying in an inn, when two great bulls began bellowing and fighting under the same roof and close to their bedroom door. This was very frail, in fact it was made of paper, so they were afraid every minute that a pair of horns would come through.

They had a trial of a different sort when they slept one night in a river boat, under the deck. The place was so low that they could not even sit up, and every now and then a sailor would wriggle in to bale the water out of the farther end of the old tub. And great big water beetles swarmed all over them in the dark. Ugh!

Which would you rather have, in the night, beetles or

bulls? I know you will say, "Neither!" I should say so too. So would the missionaries, if they could choose. They don't like such things any more than we do. But they take them as they come, and they don't mind, for the joy of carrying the Gospel to those who have never heard it.

MISSIONARY 'RITHMETIC

ARE you fond of arithmetic, I wonder? Whether our missionary liked it or not, I can't say, but he certainly had to do some very troublesome sums. It happened that he was made treasurer of the Mission, so he had to keep the accounts and pay the tradesmen, the teachers, the servants and the coolies. The money for the work came from America, but of course it had to be changed into Korean currency. One American dollar, or four English shillings, would fetch more than two thousand Korean "cash."

This sounds muddling in itself, doesn't it? For we think of "cash" as just another word for money in general. But cash over there are actual coins. The commonest piece was a brass one, about the size of a shilling, with a hole in the middle: this was five cash.

It would have been hard enough at best to account for these little bits of money, which took far more reckoning than dollars and cents, or pounds, shillings and pence. But what made it extra hard was the fact that the value of money was changing every day, going up and down like a see-saw. On Monday Mr. Underwood might change a dollar and get 3,000 cash for it; on Tuesday he might change another and get only 2,500, and on Wednesday his dollar might fetch as much as 3,500. How he ever managed to put it all down in a book and keep it straight is more than I can imagine.

A purse was no good for carrying such money as this,

for a halfpenny or a cent was worth sixty of those brass coins. In Korea and also in China people string their cash on a strong straw rope and then it is easily carried, although of course it is heavy and troublesome. Some wear it round their necks!

One day Mr. Underwood needed some change and so did the treasurer of another Mission. They could not get it in Seoul but had to fetch it from the coast, twenty-eight miles away. So these two treasurers went together. Between them they had to change three hundred dollars, or about sixty pounds, into Korean money. You may well suppose that they could not carry it back. They had to hire oxen and ponies to haul it to town.

They were not able to find enough animals to carry the whole load, so one of the missionaries took what he could get and started off with them and the other followed the next day with more beasts and the rest of the money. Twelve strong oxen were needed to bear such a weight, or else fewer oxen and some wiry little ponies thrown in. So you see it was no joke being treasurer of the Mission. I am sure when Mr. Underwood offered to go to the foreign field, he never dreamed what a deal of arithmetic he would have to do, sandwiched in between the preaching of the Gospel and various other tasks. However, it was " all in the day's work " as we sometimes say.

Building was another thing that took up a good deal of time now and then. He built a house for himself; but later on the king wanted to buy it, and so he had to build another. He also built a school and I can't say how often he helped other missionaries when they had this sort of thing to do. At first there were no good masons or carpenters and he had to oversee every bit of the work, and if he went away even for an hour or two, something was likely to go wrong. It takes a great deal of thought and care to build a house properly and sometimes a single mistake will spoil it all.

One of the most useful things Mr. Underwood ever did was to provide a seaside resort for missionaries and their children, to which they could go in the hot summer months. But by this time I ought to be calling him " Dr. Underwood " instead of " Mister." He was not at any time a doctor of medicine, although now and then he did medical work if there was a special need, but he was honoured by being made a Doctor of Divinity because of the good he had done.

Missionaries come home on furlough, as it is called, every four or five years, but often this is not much of a holiday for them as they travel from place to place, telling about the work. They need a little change every year, just like other people, but they can't come home for it, because it would cost too much. If they stayed in a hot, unhealthy city all the summer they would be likely to get ill and their children too.

In one of his trips, Dr. Underwood saw a lovely spot by the sea called Sorai, and as he walked along its firm, sandy beach, he thought to himself, " How the boys and girls would enjoy this place! How they would love to climb about these rocks! What picnics we could have on summer evenings! " Behind Sorai there is a splendid range of mountains with sharp peaks that catch the rays of the setting sun, and he said, " What grand hikes the younger missionaries could have back there and what a power of good it would do them to tramp among the hills! "

He also noticed that just above the beach there is a point of land, covered with grass, where you can sit on the top of the cliff and see the surf breaking on the rocks. From there, too, you can watch the sun set behind the mountains and the moon rise over the sea. He felt this would be the very place for missionaries to talk together in quiet over all the difficulties of their work and the problems that puzzled them—also a lovely spot to talk to God, there in His own outdoors.

Dr. Underwood was no dreamer: he was a man of

business. So he enquired what this land would cost and found it was quite cheap at the moment, because no one had happened to think what a fine place it would make.

So he bought it and sold plots to any missionaries who wished for them. They were able to put up wooden cottages at very little expense, and every summer, since Sorai was opened, a crowd of happy people have enjoyed a seaside holiday and many tired missionaries have been rested for further work.

I have been there and have picnicked on the rocks and rambled in the woods and bathed in the nice warm sea. The boys and girls have as good a time as anybody and they have reason to be grateful to Dr. Underwood for thinking out such a splendid plan and working at it till it was changed from a dream into a fact.

So you see, besides preaching the Gospel, he did arithmetic for God, whether it was keeping account of those tiresome strings of cash or working out the cost of a cottage on the beach.

THE OTHER R's

OF all the things you ever saw or heard of, which do you think is the most powerful? This is not a riddle but just a plain question. Put your hand over the page until you have answered it. A steam engine? A great gun? A stick of dynamite? An electric current?

Now shall I tell you what I think? The most powerful thing I know is printed paper. Print makes people think, and from thinking they go on to do things, whether good or bad, so print is a far greater power than even electricity. One of our poets has said, " A small drop of ink . . . makes thousands, perhaps millions, think."

Missionaries know that when they talk their voices can only reach a few people at a time, but if once they can give them the Word of God in their own language, that will be better than all the preaching they can ever do.

Mr. Underwood and his fellow-workers lost no time in setting about the translation of the Bible. It was a big task and several of them formed a Board or Committee and worked at it for years. From first to last he was its chairman.

When we read the Bible, so easily and maybe carelessly, we don't dream how much labour it cost to give it to us in our own tongue. Hundreds of years ago good and learned men toiled to put it into English, and thus did Dr. Underwood and his friends toil to translate it into Korean. They felt they must take the utmost pains not to change the meaning of a single word : for is it not the Message of God to men ? Sometimes they would spend an entire day over three or four verses of the Gospel, discussing the meaning of the Greek and how best to put that meaning into Korean.

They called to their help a few educated natives, but here they struck another difficulty. Bookish people, specially in the East, are apt to be too fond of fine language, and do not write simply enough for everyone to grasp. Now God's Word was not intended chiefly for clever folks. A great English translator once said he wished to write so plainly that any plough-boy would be able to understand. Dr. Underwood and his friends felt the same way.

Though the scholarly native helpers might easily have spoilt the Book in one way, it might have been spoilt in another way if the translators had taken their language from the talk they heard in the streets and homes. It would have been a pity if vulgar words had crept into it. You can see that this was no easy task for men who had only been a short time in the country. They had constantly to pray to be kept from mistakes and God wonderfully answered and helped them.

Dr. Underwood was always ready to attempt something new if it seemed to be needed. Knowing that, after all, most people would not read the Bible, he thought he would get out a newspaper and put the Gospel into that. He wrote to editors and printers in America to ask their advice as to how to go about it, and they gladly sent him many useful hints.

So he published a weekly paper. It contained news of the Korean court and capital that people back in the country were glad to get, tips for the farmer and the shop-keeper and articles about foreign lands. The Sunday-School lesson was there every week; there was news of the churches for which the Christians eagerly watched, and there was a column chiefly meant for the heathen, telling how our Lord Jesus is the one and only Way to God.

Koreans had not had newspapers before, and the king was very pleased with this, and had his picture taken specially for its front page. Every county magistrate had it sent him, and people of all kinds subscribed for it and read it. So they got the best News of all, sandwiched in with the news of every day.

A certain blind man had it read to him, and as he sat in the dark he pondered much over what he had heard. He learned to put his trust in the Saviour and at last he became a pastor and in spite of his handicap he was put in charge of the largest church in Korea, where he did a noble work.

You see, Dr. Underwood had a Message, and he tried in many different ways to convey that Message to the people. One September day a new idea occurred to him, as indeed they were always doing. "It will be the King's birthday this week," he said, "why not have a celebration?" At once he went off and got permission to use a big public building: then he advertised a meeting for prayer and praise, decorated the place with flags and put chairs on the platform for distinguished guests. They were needed, too. Courtiers and officials and ordinary folks flocked to the hall, to unite in keeping the King's birthday. The place was packed and hundreds were turned away.

But the real reason why Dr. Underwood held this celebration was to get a good chance of telling the people about Jesus. He sat up all night writing tracts, explaining the Gospel, and had them printed in a great hurry. The school-boys distributed them by thousands. He also wrote a hymn something like " God Save the King " which went to the same tune. All over the city the people were reading this national anthem and they said, " The new religion appears to be good. At any rate it teaches that people should be loyal to the government."

It happened that a certain man had come up from the country on business and he dropped into that meeting and was greatly interested in what he heard. He read the tracts, talked with some of the Christians and asked a good many questions. Instead of buying what he had come to town for, he bought dozens of books and a strong donkey to carry them home. When he got back he told his neighbours of his wonderful discovery and distributed the books among them. After a while, Dr. Underwood had a letter from this place, asking him to come and tell these people more about the Gospel, as a large number of them had already come to believe it.

So you see how God blesses the printed page and what a power it can be. First and chiefly, there is the Bible, His own Holy Word; but newspaper, tract and hymn-sheet may all be used to convey the Message. Paper and ink reach many more people than any voice can do, unless of course it speaks over the wireless; but few have the chance of that.

A GOOD NICK-NAME

MOST of us have nick-names, no doubt, and this is as true in the East as in the West, if not more so.

Dr. Underwood had not been very long in Korea before they called him Pul Tongari, or the Bundle of Fire. He was full of such burning enthusiasm that he seemed to carry all before him. Not only in his main business of preaching the Gospel was he so keen, but in everything he undertook. He threw himself into each fresh task with his whole heart.

To compile a dictionary is about the slowest and most tiresome bit of work that anyone can do. But a dictionary was needed, so he set to work to write it, that the new missionaries might not have such a hard time as he himself had had in studying the language. When he started to learn Korean he only had a very incomplete list of words which had been put together by someone who did not live in the country. He aimed to make things easier for those who were to follow him.

Late in life Dr. Underwood was asked to do some teaching in a College, and as by this time Japan had taken possession of Korea, the Japanese language was a great deal used. Seeing that he would have to work with Japanese government officials he thought he had better study their language. It is one of the most difficult on earth, but he was not daunted. He went over to Tokyo, entered school and set to work. Outside the regular schedule he had two teachers to coach him and altogether he put in nine hours a day studying Japanese. Of course he made very rapid progress. No wonder they called him a Bundle of Fire.

Horace Underwood, boy and man, was quick to make up his mind and equally quick to do what he felt he ought to do. He did not dawdle : he did not hum and haw. He thought swiftly ; then he acted. One day he had to make a decision in a single second, but he made it and he made it right.

In the city of Seoul there was a great deep ditch, with a stony bottom, some ten or twelve feet below the level of the street, so that two tall men could have stood in it one on the other's shoulders. Here and there it was crossed by a bridge, without any wall or parapet, and when people and ponies, oxen and sedan chairs were meeting and passing, there was not much room to spare.

Series Six   Plate Three

A Kashmir Mountain Village.

Srinagar Hospital, Kashmir.

Plate Four

Series Six

An Early Morning Congregation

One day Dr. Underwood was riding his bicycle over such a bridge and on his right there were other passengers, while on his left was the edge, with the deep ditch below. Suddenly he saw just in front of him almost under his wheel, a little child, who had darted there to get out of the way of a pony. He could not stop; he could not turn. He had to choose in an instant of time between saving the child and saving himself. Without hesitation he rode his bicycle off the bridge and crashed upon the stones below. Wonderful to say, he was not much injured. God's angels no doubt took care of him, so that he fell in such a way that he broke no bones, though he was badly shaken. It is splendid to get into such a habit of choosing the right that you will choose it when you have not a minute to think and when it is the hardest thing in the world to do.

Once, when he was spending the summer at Sorai Beach, Dr. Underwood was crossing a little ditch near his home, and he fell and broke his knee-cap for the planks were slippery from the rain. We must not say that the angels failed him that time, though. Sometimes God's children are preserved from trouble and accident and sometimes not, but whatever happens, all things work together for good to them that love Him.

Sorai was a very awkward place in which to meet with such a mishap. The patient had to be carried in a litter by six coolies and they marched two long days in drenching rain before they reached the railroad. Their way lay through "rice country," that is, there were flooded fields on either hand and they had to walk the narrow slippery paths between them. The men could scarcely keep their footing on the greasy clay and the sufferer was in constant danger of being thrown into the water. But he was a good sport, joking with the bearers and trying to cheer his anxious son.

If you want more stories about this fine British-American missionary you must look for them in a larger book. For thirty-one years he served God in Korea, and all through the country Pastor Wun-too-oo, as he was called, was honoured and loved. That was the native way of pronouncing Underwood and it made not a bad name at all, for " Wun " means " Chief " and a brave Chief he was.

He lived to see multitudes confess Jesus as their Saviour and knew that his own work and that of his fellow-missionaries had been wonderfully blessed by God. The Christians proved very earnest in spreading the Gospel; that story of We Ju, which you remember, was only one of many such. Most of the people were poor and could not give much money for the work, but they gave their time and labour, which was better still. At their yearly Bible Conferences they would have a subscription list of days instead of cash, and they would promise one day, two days, a week or a fortnight, according as they were able. Then for that time, during the season when farm work was slack, they would go out into the highways and byways and tell the Good News of salvation.

At last Dr. Underwood, the well-beloved Pastor Wun-too-oo, was called up higher. He had fought the good fight, finished the course, and kept the faith, so he went in to see the King.

As you think of his splendid life and the lives of all the great men and women of whom you have heard and read, remember this: the Lord Jesus is just as ready to undertake *your* life as any other and He will use it in His service, if you simply give your heart to Him and accept Him as your Saviour and your Lord.

ARTHUR NEVE OF KASHMIR
GETTING READY

COULD you find out whether your grandmother has such a thing as a Cashmere shawl? There are not many to be seen nowadays, but once they were very fashionable and the best of them cost as much as a hundred pounds apiece. They were made from the fine, long fleece of the mountain goat, spun by Indian women and woven on rough hand-looms by the clever weavers of Cashmere. About half a century ago there came a famine which drove these people from their homes and their industry came almost to an end.

The shawls, you see, were named from the country from which they came. To-day it is generally spelt Kashmir. You can easily find it on the map if you bear in mind that at its top left-hand corner, India, China, and Afghanistan meet.

Central Asia is sometimes called the Roof of the World, because of its massive mountain ranges, and Kashmir is the most northerly native state of India, just on the edge of this roof. It is a lovely country and travellers have written interesting accounts of it.

This story is about Arthur Neve. He enjoyed mountain climbing and he was also fond of sketching and liked to sit down and paint a beautiful scene before he left it, but it was not for sport or for art that he went to Kashmir. He was a medical missionary and went there to bring health to the sick and sight to the blind, and best of all to give them the Gospel of the Lord Jesus.

Now that you have been introduced to him, no doubt you are ready to begin at the beginning and hear all about him.

His first home was at Brighton and there he and his brothers and sisters enjoyed all the delights of the seaside, bathing and boating and fishing to their hearts' content. The boys went to the Grammar School and Arthur was a steady student if not specially brilliant.

After a time the Neves moved into the country, to a large house near the Downs, with beautiful grounds round it. They were never tired of rambling over those hills, which give you such a glorious feeling of heaps of room and nothing to hinder you or hem you in. Blue sky above, short grass below, clumps of gorse here and there, nothing else to be seen but perhaps a flock of sheep, nothing to be heard but the lark singing overhead.

They had their ponies too, so could go far afield when they felt like it, and now and then picnic in one of the old ruins for which Sussex is famous. Its castles go back to the time of the Normans and there are even hints of Roman remains.

But after all, the oldest relics are young compared with the treasures of the rocks, which tell the history of the age-long past to those who know how to read it. Their father explained to them how the chalk of which the cliffs and Downs are made is largely formed of the shells of tiny creatures. They have mostly been ground to powder but sometimes you come across sea-urchin's shells or the skeleton of an ancient cuttle-fish, or a fossil beautifully shaped like a ram's horn. It was in the big chalk-pits that the children got their best finds.

Indoors there were plenty of interesting books and best of all they loved travel stories, specially those about Africa. Their chief hero was David Livingstone, the great explorer and splendid missionary, who was then opening up the Dark Continent, and blazing a trail for others to follow. Arthur was about fourteen when one day the news came that Livingstone had been found dead in his little hut, kneeling as though in prayer. The boy wished he could go to Africa and fight against the cruel slave trade as did that great man.

The whole Neve family were very keen about sending the Gospel to heathen lands. Father and mother and children all felt there was nothing in the world so thrilling as this great enterprise. Before many years had passed three of the boys went out as missionaries. But preparation had to come first, and hard preparation at that, for Arthur and his younger brother Ernest decided to be doctors and that means long training.

Arthur went to Edinburgh University and was joined by his brother two years later. He did very well in his medical classes and took a number of medals and prizes. But no one could call him a book-worm: he had time for other things besides study.

Whatever he did, he did with all his might. A fellow missionary said of him many years later, " He was ready to join in any sport going . . . . In games he played most energetically and always for his side rather than to draw attention to his own prowess : his great delight appeared to be to see the good play of others."

When he was in his second year in College news came from Africa which made him want more than ever to go there. Stanley, the explorer who some time before had gone out to look for Livingstone and had found him in the forest, sent an urgent message home. He said that missionary recruits were needed for Uganda, as a powerful chief was willing to receive them and allow them to teach his people. Very soon eight volunteered and went out, but in a short time the spears of savages and the deadly fever had killed half the little party. This bad news did not frighten Arthur Neve, however. He longed to go and fill one of the gaps, but for the time being he had to stick to his studies and get thoroughly prepared for the great work.

All good missionaries begin at home. When Neve was attending Edinburgh University, he and other students worked among the poor in the slums of the city. There they put into practice their medical knowledge and at the same time they held Gospel meetings for the grown-ups and Sunday School for the children. There was so much to do that it kept them very busy in their spare time. Neve, when he had passed his examinations, worked in the Edinburgh Infirmary and gained the experience that every doctor must have before he can start alone in a new country.

He had by this time written to the Church Missionary Society and offered to go to Uganda. But just then he seemed to be still more needed somewhere else. The Society asked him to go, not to Africa, but to Kashmir, and believing this to be the call of God, he willingly gave up his own plans and set his face in a new direction. As a true soldier of Christ his one thought was to obey his Captain, not to pick and choose for himself.

ON THE WAY

Bombay, the gateway of India, is a great city with broad thoroughfares and splendid public buildings. People from all parts of the world gather here and about forty different languages may be heard upon the streets. One evening Arthur Neve went with a friend to an open air meeting and there he gave his first witness for Jesus in the new country. It was in English, of course, but he noticed that the Indians seemed to understand.

The next few weeks he spent in visiting a number of mission stations and seeing the country. It is quite easy to get about in India for the train service is good. We take our own bedding with us and spread it out upon the seat at night. On one of his trips, however, the doctor had the new experience of riding an elephant.

He could not go at once to Kashmir because the mountains

were blocked with snow. So he stayed for some months in the big city of Amritzar in the Punjab, which was then the headquarters of the Church Missionary Society. It is a very busy place. Here traders gather from every town in the north of India : there are merchants from Afghanistan, pilgrims from Central Asia and fierce-looking tribesmen from the mountains.

Arthur Neve spent most of his time in studying the language. India is a country of many languages : the one he had to learn was Urdu which is spoken chiefly in the north. But he was soon called upon for medical service, for cholera broke out in the city and the government doctor was ill, so that Neve had to take his place.

Early in February, that is, while it was still winter and the mountain roads were not open, he had a letter from the missionary in Kashmir whose colleague he was going to be. It said he was ill and not able to get about to do his work. Young Neve was a good sport and he felt at once that although it might be risky he must somehow try and get up there without delay.

To reach Kashmir you take the train as far as Rawalpindi. I could take you that far, for I have been there myself, and seen the Himalayas in the distance, covered with snow. But it is after one leaves the train that the thrill of the journey begins. There was what they call a " tonga road " as far as a certain hill-station. The tonga is a light, two-wheeled cart that carries the mails, but it was not running at that time of year, so the doctor rode his own trusty pony.

Taking short cuts, scrambling up the hill-sides, crawling under the branches, he reached the hill-station and went to the bungalow where travellers usually stay. It was shut up and the other houses, too, were swathed with mats, to keep the snow from blocking the chimneys and coming in at the windows. " This village is in curl-papers and night-caps," he thought to himself, " and more than half asleep."

He was just wondering what to do when a tall man came

striding down the hill, who turned out to be a fellow-Briton. The doctor told him what a fix he was in and at once the other said he must come and stay at the Club, which he gladly did.

When he left there it was down hill all the way, and gradually he dropped from those snowy heights to a tropical valley, where bananas and date-palms were growing. They were just making a cart-road into Kashmir, but this was a bad time to use it. The old bridle-path had been blasted away by dynamite, and as yet there were only short bits of the new. So Neve had neither the one nor the other and had to wind his way up and down the mountains as best he could and take some pretty dangerous paths.

One day he paused for an hour to take a sketch, and on catching up with the rest he saw his clothes, books and medicines lying scattered in a deep gulley, while a lot of his oranges were floating down the river, going back the way he had come. The narrow path along the side of the cliff was more crumbly than they had supposed. The baggage pony's hind legs broke it away and he only saved himself by a great struggle, while his load fell off and rolled to the bottom.

Day by day the scenery grew wilder and more glorious and Arthur Neve immensely enjoyed riding his pony at the head of his own caravan. In the thickets he saw strange birds. There was the orange bullfinch, a very gay fellow and a loud singer, and the bird of paradise fly-catcher, with a long, waving, silvery tail.

Now and then monkeys scrambled along the banks or swung themselves from branch to branch, picking the berries as they went. If any of the men tried to hit them they soon showed that they knew how to hit back.

Further on there was a heavy fall of snow. It was knee-deep in fact, and they had to look out for avalanches. They could see them tumbling every now and then down the mountain-side and breaking into spray as they fell. When the sun came out upon the snow this Jhelum Valley was like fairyland. One afternoon the path suddenly opened upon a most wonderful view. They could see for about fifty miles. Down below lay a beautiful lake with the mountains and glaciers reflected in its waters and around it green fields and dozens of little villages. The doctor stood a long time looking at the splendid scene, and wondering what lay beyond those snow-capped peaks.

The last lap of the journey was done by boat, first down the Jhelum, then across the Wular Lake, and finally up the river to the city of Srinagar, the capital of Kashmir, and the people to whom this young doctor was to give his life. The old doctor met him at the landing-place and I need scarcely say that he was very glad to see him.

Don't forget that in all parts of the world there are splendid men and women who have worn out in the service of Christ, and they are waiting for young ones to come and take their places. You may not be able as yet to offer to a missionary society but you might offer in your heart to the Lord Jesus. Perhaps you could say in the words of the hymn :

> " Just as I am, young, strong and free,
> To be the best that I can be
> For truth, and righteousness and Thee,
> Lord of my life, I come."

THE CITY OF THE SUN

The name of Kashmir's capital, the goal of Arthur Neve's long journey, is a poser, isn't it? Srinagar : how shall we pronounce it? Well, first say slowly, Sirin-ug-gar, then try and slur that first " i " and say it quickly, as though you were going to sneeze, Srinagar.

Srinagar has been called by Orientals the City of the Sun. Europeans often speak of it as the Venice of the East. No doubt you understand what that means, for you have seen pictures of Venice and you know that canals there take the place of streets, and people travel by boat instead of by motor cars and buses.

We have seen how the doctor came by boat across the Wular Lake and up the River Jhelum. The city has another and smaller lake of its own, connected with it by many canals. It is very beautiful and is dotted with many islands where willow trees bend over tall waving rushes, and the water is so clear that you can see the trout swimming down below.

Kingfishers and golden aureoles flit among the trees, and heavily laden punts move silently across the water, bringing vegetables and fruit from the floating gardens. These are a clever dodge of the Kashmiris. They bind together the growing rushes, cut them loose below and throw some soil on top and there they put hundreds of young plants, which, with the hot sun and plentiful moisture, come on very fast.

While the lake is lovely, the city itself is crowded and dirty. Many stuffy courts and alleys line its network of canals. Still, it is quaintly interesting, for no two houses are alike and they are dotted about on the river banks in a happy-go-lucky fashion. The rich have their fine mansions and the poor their shabby shacks, sometimes the woodwork is curiously carved or there may be a roomy balcony reaching out over the water.

When visitors first see the city they wonder what is the matter with it and ask if there has been a bombardment or an earthquake for so many of the buildings are crooked, or broken down. But this is simply because the Kashmiris have not learned to build straight, and are rather careless about mending.

The most surprising thing of all is to see grass and flowers growing on the roofs, and sheep and goats feeding up there. This happens because these roofs are made of mud and are not so sloping as ours. The worst of it is that they are very heavy and sometimes after a fall of snow they will cave in and kill the inmates in their sleep. To prevent this misfortune people have a trap-door in the ceiling and so can go up and shovel off the snow, likely enough on the heads of the passers-by.

In some of the narrow streets the upper storeys of the houses lean over so far that the roofs nearly meet, and now and then beams are put between them to keep them apart. The different trades and crafts have their own quarters, the silversmiths are in one district and the woodcarvers in another. In many of the bazaars you may see men making the things they sell. The saddlers are working, not on leather but on cloth, for the Mohammedans would not use a saddle of pigskin, and the Hindus object to all leather.

In some of the shops men and boys are doing embroidery in bright colours, with silk or wool, and their work is most artistic. A great din comes from the quarters of the coppersmiths, where they make beautiful jugs and basins and also a very curious thing called a duck, because it is shaped like one. It is filled with water and put on the fire, and when the water boils the steam blows up the fire. Quite a clever scheme!

Early in the morning the milkmen come running in from the villages round about, each with three earthenware pots upon his head, one on top of the other. It is a wonder they can balance such a weight and scarcely ever have a spill. Women, too, carry a great deal on their heads, such as their cooking vessels and their washing and they walk with a special grace in consequence of this habit.

Up and down the river, on the canals and on the lake, are many house-boats in which whole families live. There the women cook the rice and the children play, the grandmother sits at her spinning-wheel and the menfolk smoke their long pipes or hookahs.

In speaking of the dwellers in the city we must not forget the dogs. There are thousands of them and they are very wild, as they belong to nobody and have a hard time trying to pick up a living. In summer they often go mad and in winter they are savage because they are starving, poor things. They eat up the garbage in the streets and but for them there would no doubt be much more sickness than there is, for they make good scavengers.

There is one very strange thing about these dogs. Although they have no homes, they divide themselves up into parties and each party has its own district. If any dog ventures into a district not his own he gets badly punished. As for an English dog, if he is so unlucky as to find himself alone upon the streets he stands no chance at all.

Now let us close our eyes and try to imagine the city to which Arthur Neve had come. A circle of snow-capped mountains frames the picture. Then, down the middle of it is the River Jhelum, winding its way under seven bridges. We see the houses of all sorts and sizes lining the water-side, the canals thronged with boats, the narrow streets, the grass-covered roofs, the over-hanging balconies, the noisy bazaars, the quarrelsome dogs.

We also see the handsome mosque where the Mohammedans worship, from one of whose minarets there sounds five times a day the call to prayer. Here and there we notice a Hindu temple, with its roof of gilt or tin shining in the sun. But how happy we are to see also the Christian Church, the Mission Schools and the Hospital, where many people, men, women and children, have learned to know the true God and our Saviour Jesus Christ.

A GREAT UNDERTAKING

While Kashmir is one of the most beautiful regions in the world and its climate is healthy, there is nevertheless a great deal of sickness and doctors are badly needed.

The people are more nearly related to our own race than most Orientals and some of them might easily be taken for

Europeans, for they have a fair skin and rosy cheeks. The women are often beautiful. But they have not learned to take proper care of their bodies, and the things you have been taught at home and at school about health and hygiene they have never heard. They don't get enough fresh air, at any rate in the towns. Living in stuffy courts and alleys and bending over their work, they become weak and consumptive. They don't go in for games and get scarcely any exercise. Because of the dirt and the ignorance, disease quickly spreads and there are epidemics of smallpox and typhus and cholera and plague which kill them by the thousand.

Most of them know nothing about germs and see no reason why sick people should be separated from the rest. The Mohammedans when they are ill just say, " It is the will of Allah," and the Hindus think some deity, such as the Goddess of Smallpox, has brought the disease. They even pretend to welcome her, because they think it dangerous to offend her. They don't like to be vaccinated. Their forefathers never dreamed of such a thing, they say, and why should they do it? Some of them are learning by degrees, but it takes time to teach a whole people. I wish you could read the story of the Boys' High School. You will find it in " Fifty Years Against the Stream " by the Rev. C. E. Tyndale-Biscoe. In this school and under this missionary, fellows who were lazy and proud have learned to help themselves and others. They have done splendid work in fighting cholera and cleaning up their city. They have also become fine athletes and done much life-saving upon the Lake.

The country folk are healthier than the dwellers in the towns for they live and work out of doors. But they don't understand that we must have fresh air by night as well as by day. In winter time they bring the cows in and let them have the lower rooms and the family live upstairs. They stop up every hole and cranny with mud and straw and the heat from the cows rises up from below and keeps them all warm. This may be cosy and cheap but it is far from wholesome.

When we are ill we send for the doctor and very soon he is on the spot. In Kashmir they cannot do that and indeed in India as a whole probably not more than one person in ten is within easy reach of a fully trained man. The native doctors often do the patients more harm than good, set their bones wrongly, dress their sores in a dirty way, or give them medicines that are worse than useless. Kashmir is as large as England and Wales but it has only a handful of trained doctors, so nearly half of the boys and girls who are born in this beautiful land die while they are still little, just through lack of knowledge on the part of their parents, and lack of a doctor in time of need.

This will give you some slight idea what a blessing a Mission Hospital must be, with its wise physicians and skilled nurses and the kindness that makes every patient feel happy and at home.

When missionaries first went to Kashmir the Governor of Srinagar did not want them there and did everything possible to hinder their work. A medical missionary, Dr. Elmslie, spent one summer in the country and more than two thousand people came to see him, but when he tried to hire a house he was told that he could not have one. These were the Governor's orders. However, he was not the sort of man to give up, so he built two wooden huts and had a tent besides and thus he began the hospital which has since become famous.

By degrees the officials left off annoying and persecuting the missionaries, for everybody could see what a splendid work they were doing. There was a terrible famine in Kashmir and people had to eat roots and grasses, chaff instead of corn and even the bark off the trees. Thousands of them died of starvation and then there came the awful pestilence and carried away thousands more. At this time of trouble it was the missionaries who made plans for relief, gave out food, nursed the sick and provided for orphan boys and girls.

The doctor who was in charge of all this effort broke down ; he carried on until he could do so no longer. This was the man whom Arthur Neve went to relieve, you remember, travelling by his pony through the snowy passes before the road was open for regular traffic.

Dr. Neve was very much struck with all that Dr. Downes had done, with no one to help him except the Kashmiri men he himself had trained. But the buildings gave him rather a shock. Here in England we are accustomed to well-built hospitals, fitted with everything the doctors can need, and kept spick and span from roof to basement. This mission hospital consisted of a few sheds, with mud floors, mud walls, and mud roofs. In one of them, indeed, the walls were only four feet high and the rest of the space up to the ceiling was open to wind and rain.

Such as it was, however, this hospital was in a fine position. Just outside Srinagar is a bold and rocky hill, and near its base there runs out a grassy spur, ending in steep reddish cliffs. When the missionaries were doing the famine relief work they had a broad terrace cut right across the front of the hill. These men thought ahead, you see ; they pictured what would be needed in the future. That is the kind of men that are wanted in the mission field, men with business heads as well as Christian hearts.

So when Dr. Arthur Neve arrived on the scene, he found a grand spot in which to begin work, but no hospital wards worthy of the name. Rome was not built in a day. The doctors who came before him had made a good start ; that was all they could do.

Perhaps you remember that a younger brother, Ernest, was with Arthur at Edinburgh University, and part of their time they were in training together. Now Ernest came out to Srinagar and the two set to work to rebuild the hospital, while all the time caring for the sick in the old sheds and doing operations in the midst of difficult surroundings. The well-to-do paid fees and they put these aside for the building. Others brought gifts, for they had come to understand that this work was being done purely for the good of Kashmir.

After eight years the two young doctors saw their dream come true. The new hospital was complete, with handsome towers, broad verandahs and red gables, a fine group of buildings stretching along the beautiful hill-side.

Inside, the wards were clean and bright, the walls painted a pale green and the floors polished. The neat iron bedsteads were a great improvement on the Indian string beds and the white sheets and scarlet blankets looked very smart. Many patients were able to live out on the verandah, where they could enjoy the roses in their season blooming around them, and have a peep of the green lawn beyond.

How happy those two doctors must have been! It had taken years of hard work to bring about this result, but it was a thousand times worth while.

Every one of the mission hospitals requires a deal of money to run it, and if some people did not make efforts and sacrifices they would have to be closed. Those who cannot go out as missionaries may send their gifts and so help to carry on the work. If we offer what we can to the Lord Jesus Himself He will accept it whether it be little or much. He is still watching what people give, just as when He sat in the Temple and saw the widow drop her two mites into the treasury.

IN THE HOSPITAL

It is not the buildings, though, that you chiefly want to see, but rather the Kashmir people who are patients there, particularly the boys and girls lying out on the verandahs, getting well as fast as they can and ready to give you a smile as you pass. I can't say whom you would see if you went there this minute, but I can tell you a story of a young patient who was much frightened when she was carried in and was very sorry when it was time to leave.

Zuni was a pretty little girl nine years old, with her hair in plaits down her back. Her father was dead and her mother was never well, so she had a great deal to do. She fed the cow, the sheep and the fowls, and looked after her baby brother. When wood was needed, it was Zuni who went to the forest, and gathered it and dragged the heavy load home. One day when she was doing this she knocked her leg against the stump of a tree. It hurt a good deal but she thought it would be all right in a day or two. Instead of getting better, though, it became badly swollen and soon she could not walk at all.

Her mother did not send for the native doctor because she could not afford to pay him, and Zuni got worse and worse. Very likely if he had come he would have done her more harm than good. One day a neighbour said, " Why don't you take her to the city, to that hospital on the hill ? " But it was two days' journey away and how could they dare undertake such a trip ? Besides, they did not know what might be done to Zuni once she got inside that place. A little boy who lived not far from them had been there, and left one of his legs behind. He said they were very good to him and gave him plenty to eat, and took away the pain, so that now he could manage quite nicely with a crutch. But Zuni was terrified and begged her mother not to take her to the foreigners.

However, she got worse and worse and it became plain that if something were not done she would soon die. Her grandmother had been to Srinagar and had visited the hospital and seen how kind everybody was, and she said Zuni really must go at once. As her mother was not well enough to travel, her aunt took her. They hired a boat and made their way along the winding river until they saw the city in the distance, with the row of hospital buildings on the cliff and the red cross flag floating in the breeze.

Zuni's aunt carried her out of the boat, and up the hill to a room where a crowd of people were waiting to see the doctor. Someone read to them out of a little book about a Man who went about doing good and healing everybody who came to Him. Zuni wished she could go to Him herself. But she had not much time to think, for soon a little bell rang, and she was told it was her turn to pass into the next room and see the doctor.

She was very frightened and her aunt was a bit frightened too. They both wondered if he would cut off her leg as he had done the little boy's. He said he would put her to sleep and soon she would be all right. When she woke up she found herself in a nice white bed, such a bed as she had never even seen before, much less slept in. And in the next one there was another little girl, who like herself had come from the mountains. So she very soon felt at home.

Sometimes the nurses, when they had a few minutes to spare, would sit and sing to them, or teach them a text. But what they most enjoyed was to hear the wonderful stories from the Bible, while someone with a magic lantern threw lovely pictures upon the wall. Thus these little girls learned about Jesus and how He not only healed the sick and the blind, as they had heard in the waiting-room, but died for our sins upon the Cross.

Zuni's leg was cured and she became well and strong. At last the day came when she had to leave that delightful place, go round the garden for the last time, say good-bye to the doctor and the nurses and her little friends and start for home. Once more she had to take up her task, feed the cow and the sheep and the fowls, gather the wood, look after her little brother and help her sick mother. I wish I could tell you the rest of her story but I don't know any more. Whether she remembered what she had learned and told the neighbours about Jesus, I cannot say. But this I do know : we ought to pray for those who go as patients into our Mission hospitals that they may not forget what they learn there. We at home go to church and Sunday School all the year round; they perhaps have only a few weeks of teaching and nobody to help them once they have returned to their village.

People in that part of the world don't go to the doctor as soon as they are ill. They try everything else first, and usually make themselves worse and only call on the missionary when everyone else has failed, and when it may be too late. They put off going if it is a busy season in the fields, or if it is not convenient for their relatives to go with them. So when there is a fair or a great religious festival, many patients come to the hospital, not because they all happen to get ill at once, but because they have been waiting for a chance to come. On one day in this hospital at Srinagar the doctors saw more than four hundred patients, and while they were waiting for their turns they all heard something of the Gospel.

Even if they only tell a very little when they get home, the Good News is spread, for the sick people lying in the wards at one time may come from a hundred different villages and towns. Besides, their relatives sit with them day after day, and what one forgets another may remember. The Mohammedans who believe in one God but do not know his Son, the Hindus who worship idols, the Tibetans who are Buddhists and pray by turning a wheel, sit side by side and hear the same story, the old, old story of Jesus and His love.

I wish I could give you some idea of how many people attend this one hospital in a year. Suppose they stood two and two, like a school "crocodile," rather close together, how far do you think they would reach? Ten miles. Now you can probably mention some village or town ten miles from your home. Try to imagine a procession closely packed, reaching that far. Each one is treated separately with kindness and skill. Think how much medicine is needed for them all! And how many bandages for the surgical cases! Why, this hospital uses up twenty-five miles of bandage in a year.

The Kashmiris often seem surprised at the kindness shown

to them. They are not used to it. They say, "Neither father nor mother would do as much for us as you do." Then someone tells them how God loves them and how Jesus died for them, and they find it possible to believe this because they have seen His love in the faces of His servants and felt it in their gentle touch.

THE KASHMIR EARTHQUAKE

It was five o'clock one cold, drizzly morning in May, and Dr. Neve was lying awake for it was too soon to get up. Suddenly the house shook and there was a very queer feeling of twisting and turning and he knew it was an earthquake. He waited half a minute wondering if it was already over, or going to be worse. The noise increased, the timbers of the roof creaked, the doors swung open, the pictures shook and bricks and plaster came falling down the staircase. It was still almost dark so he could not see very much from his window. But what he heard was terrible, for up from the city there rose a scream of fear and pain from thousands of voices at once.

It did not take him very long to put on his clothes. He sent over to the hospital for a quantity of splints, dressings and bandages, and picking up a few helpers he started for the city to see what he could do.

The soldiers' barracks had fallen down and already hundreds of men were digging away the heavy mud roofs, lifting the timbers and rescuing those who were pinned beneath them. Many, however, were dead and others were too badly hurt for any help. Part of the palace also had collapsed and other large buildings. The doctor was surprised that not more houses had fallen. As you will remember, many of them are out of the straight and very tumble-down in appearance. These very ones, however, stood up, while those which looked firmer fell down. This was partly because they were largely made of wood, and the beams were well jointed, so that a house even four storeys high swayed in one piece, as it were, and did not fall apart and break up.

While the doctors were busy attending to the injured in Srinagar they learned that two other towns had been almost wiped out, and decided that they must try to do something for them also. So Dr. Neve got a boat and went several days' journey down the river and while he treated those on the spot his helpers scoured the villages round about and brought fresh cases in. Everything had been so badly shaken that there was no safe building in which to work, so they put up tents and hired some big barges and filled them all with patients. From ten miles round people brought their friends to the doctor, sometimes carrying them on their shoulders and sometimes bringing bed and all, like the four men in the Gospel. For a whole week there were earthquakes every day, for the land was settling itself after the shock. In one hamlet the doctor found the forest trees lying in heaps and pointing in every direction except the sky, and down below he saw a pit like a deserted quarry, with the ruins of little homes sticking up here and there. In this landslide only seven of the forty-seven villagers escaped with their lives.

Dr. Neve did all that he could for the country folk, setting broken limbs, and dressing wounds and burns and then he returned to the city to look after the people there. When winter came he managed to get off again for a little while and paid a flying visit to his earthquake patients in these towns and villages. He went in a small boat but here and there he had to get out and walk, for the river was frozen in places and there was ice for miles all round the Lake. He carried a tiny charcoal stove to warm his cabin, and he cooked his meals over it, porridge and eggs and such like, for he was a handy man, this doctor.

Before he reached the rapids he had to change into a flat-bottomed boat. Down the broad, swirling river they went, faster and faster, every now and then skirting a whirlpool where the men had to paddle hard to keep the boat straight ahead. One moment they were meeting rough waves which broke on board and the next perhaps they came to a shallow place where they bumped over the stones.

On this trip the doctor carried a hundred and twenty little coats for needy boys and girls. He came to a certain large village which had been newly built after the earthquake and here they gave him a room which had been cleared of everything except smoke. Hearing that he had arrived, little naked children came paddling through the snow and slush, their teeth chattering with the cold. They dropped in at his window, and funniest of all, they popped up through a hole in the floor. He loved the children and longed to help them every one, but he saw that some of the grown-ups were greedy and tried to get more than their share, and they sent the little ones in without clothes just to touch his heart. It was hard to know what to do, for they all looked alike in their birthday suits and he could not tell which were really in want.

This trip was extra work for the doctor and he had to squeeze it in as best he could. Missionaries often have such extras. In times of special trouble, such as an earthquake or fire, or an epidemic of cholera or plague they prove themselves to be the true friends of the people. Everybody can see that they not only preach the Glad Tidings of the Gospel but they are ready to help in every way, to feed the hungry and clothe the naked and heal the sick. All this unselfish service makes people more ready to believe in the love of God of which they try to tell.

CAMPING OUT

Zuni, you will remember, went to the hospital by boat, and so do many patients. It is fairly easy even if the way be long. But those who live in the mountain villages, far away from the river side cannot manage to get to the city, specially if they happen to be lame or blind. So the missionary doctor, when he can spare the time, will take a trip into those out of the way parts, carrying his medicine chest and his surgical instruments.

When Dr. Neve did this he made the first part of the journey in a flat-bottomed boat, very long and narrow, with a roof and walls of matting. Two or three Kashmiri men, harnessed to a rope, walked on the river bank and pulled the boat along. They passed many a little village where men were fishing and women were pounding rice or spinning in front of their homes. When they reached the big lake they paddled the boat across, and that without losing any time for the storms come down so suddenly.

Once on the other side, they started to cross the mountains. The doctor had to engage porters to carry the baggage and then the climb began. When they reached the top of the pass and looked back, they saw the lovely Vale of Kashmir stretching out below with the lake shining in the sun.

Try and picture them now as they press forward, mountains all around them with snowfields in their hollows, dense forests of pine and spruce where wild beasts have their haunts. Now they come to a little village, where the Indian corn has just been gathered in. Heaps of yellow cobs are lying on the terraced slopes. The people have heard that the great doctor has come from the city, and they quickly bring their sick and blind and perhaps one or two cases of broken bones which have never been properly set. The doctor chooses a large walnut-tree and spreading a table in its shade, he sets out his bottles and instruments. By this time the crowd has gathered and he makes them all sit down, while he tells the story of the Gospel which some of them have never heard before. He says they can learn more of it from his little books of which they can buy a copy for about a farthing, but unfortunately very few of them can read.

After the service the sick people come up to the table one by one and he gives them medicine and advice or perhaps does some small operation. He will probably attend to quite a hundred in a day.

The herdsmen of the mountains are called gujars. They have big flocks of goats and herds of buffaloes and they move from one grassy spot to another, living in tents or little huts made of boughs. They are quiet, kindly people. For the most part they dress in dark blue cotton with a red stripe in it and the women are fond of wearing bead necklaces, silver chains and bright-coloured bracelets.

One day a procession of these gujars came to the doctor's camp carrying a stretcher of branches with a little boy upon it. He had been mauled by a big, black bear, when following the herd home through the forest. If the doctor had not come along just then, the little chap would soon have been dead. He had him carried down to the lake and then by boat to the hospital and soon he was well again and able to go home.

We read in the Gospel that the Lord Jesus went about doing good, and healing those who were sick of divers diseases. Our medical missionaries try closely to follow the Master and wherever they go they leave health and happiness behind. Can you imagine a more beautiful life than this?

A HOME FOR THE HOMELESS

Among the patients who attended the hospital every now and then there would come a leper. There are many such afflicted people in the East but in our own country we do not see them, so we are apt to forget that there is such a thing as leprosy in the world to-day. We read about it in the Bible and we know how the leper was an outcast, and when meeting others on the road, he had to call out a warning, in the terrible words, " Unclean, unclean ! "

Many lepers are not dangerous, any more than people who are marked with small-pox. They have had the disease and it has burnt itself out. But others are a very great menace and in India they are not kept separate. They can work at any trade and even sell food. The milkman may be a leper. They travel on the train, the ox-cart or the camel-cart like other people and they sleep in the public rest-houses. Wherever they go they leave germs behind. When men sit in a circle smoking, they pass the pipe or hookah from one to another, and this is a dirty and unhealthy habit at the best, and very dangerous if such a leper is in the group.

While these poor sufferers may have the disease for years and not be interfered with, when they get so bad that it is unpleasant for their neighbours they are often driven from the village and have to pick up a living by the roadside. Dr. Arthur Neve and his brother Ernest tried to help those who came to the gate of the hospital. They could at least dress their sores and give them food to eat. For some they did more than this. They took them in and set a ward apart for their use.

In recent years a medicine has been prepared which will cure many cases if they are taken in time. This drug was known centuries ago but for certain reasons it could not be used. Now it is proving to be a great blessing.

The two Neves often wished they could have a separate place for the lepers, where they could be well cared for and not be a danger to other people. One day they went out together and hunted for a good spot. You remember the beautiful Dal Lake close to the city of Srinagar. On one side of it they found a little peninsula jutting out into the water, with a ruined house upon it, standing on higher ground. On making enquiries they learned that this was an old powder factory belonging to the Kashmir army. They asked the Maharajah to give them this land and he willingly did so and also a sum of money to put up their first buildings.

It is now a very lovely place and indeed some say it is the most beautifully situated leper colony in the world. On three sides there are the blue waters of the lake and in its little creeks there grow the pink lotus and the pure white water-lily. In spring time the whole place is bright with apple blossom, also almond and cherry and plum. And behind all there is the circle of snow-capped mountains.

Here poor lepers who have perhaps been turned out of their villages find a happy home and they can have a little garden of their own if they care to cultivate it. They hear of the love of Jesus and learn that the One who touched and healed the lepers in Palestine long ago has sent His servants to heal and help them in India to-day.

IN LITTLE TIBET

That little-known region of central Asia that we call the Roof of the World stretches on its eastern side into Tibet, a country which travellers visit at their peril and where missionaries are not allowed to live. Nearly a century ago the Kashmiris conquered a part of Tibet and added it to their own country. It still goes by the name of Little Tibet, or Ladak, although it is now a part of India. Its capital is Leh. If you take your map and turn to Kashmir, put your finger on Srinagar, and draw it along due east, you will come to Leh.

Between these two there are many ups and downs and when Dr. Neve went to Ladak he did some stiff mountain climbing and had narrow escapes walking among the glaciers and along the edge of steep precipices. He carried his scientific instruments with him to make observations for he was something of an explorer as well as a doctor.

Rivers had to be crossed, sometimes by means of very frail bridges and sometimes without any at all. When they were not too deep he and his men could wade across, but it was not easy with laden ponies. One man would take a pony's head and another would hang on to his tail and so pull him through. Or perhaps they would come to a bridge which they were told animals must not cross with their loads. Then the men had to take these off and carry them themselves, no doubt wondering whether they would come to grief in the middle. The most tricky thing of all was the rope bridge. This is made of three ropes of hazel twigs, one for the feet to walk on and two for the hands to hold on by. When there is a strong wind blowing and a river raging underneath, the traveller does not greatly enjoy the crossing.

Sometimes the doctor came to the ruins of an old castle or fort perched high on some rocky hill and he was reminded of the wars of ancient times when the people of Ladak fought to keep out the invader.

More interesting still were the mountains themselves. The peaks stood so tall and straight, one above another, like the pipes of a vast organ. The strangest thing about them was their colour, for each pipe was different from the rest. They were pale green, purple and yellow, grey, orange and chocolate, varying with the rocks of which they were built.

When climbing a difficult pass the doctor rode a yak, for this animal can travel where a pony cannot go. It is a sort of ox with long, shaggy hair, bushy tail and very large horns. The yak has a fierce, wild look and an alarming habit of gnashing its teeth. For this reason it has been named the grunting bison. Large herds roam wild in Ladak on the broad plateaux. Those which are bred by the inhabitants are smaller than the wild sort, but strong and very useful as carriers. They manage to pick up a living on the desert, where there is next to nothing to eat and what there is may be covered with snow. The doctor was glad of them in crossing the mountains for they are so sure-footed, and even among the loose stones on a dangerous path they do not slip. He did not have a saddle and bridle but sat on a folded blanket and held on by the yak's mane.

One day they came to a strange looking building in an

equally strange looking place. It was a Buddhist monastery and the rock on which it stood was a bright yellow, its natural colour. A river had cut its way through walls of rock forming steep cliffs and fantastic pinnacles.

The monks had bridged over the hollows and clefts with balconies of carved woodwork and here and there they had made curious monuments. It was all very weird. Let into the wall of the terrace were nearly a hundred little prayer-wheels, and as the monks walked back and forth they set them going. Some prayer-wheels are turned by water, others by the wind, but it is considered a great merit to turn them by hand.

Inside the wheel there is a paper with a prayer written on it, though usually it is just one sentence, which is more like an exclamation than a prayer, " Om mane padme hum." It means, " Oh, the jewel in the lotus flower," and for most people it might as well have no meaning at all. The Tibetans think that if they repeat these syllables millions of times over they will be reckoned righteous people and it will be to their credit in the next world.

To us it seems very sad that any one should have such a wrong idea of prayer and should not understand that we can come to God and speak naturally to Him, as we should to our earthly father. Yet even in our Christian country there are many who gabble and mumble their prayers as though the words had no more meaning than " Om mane padme hum." Often in asking a blessing at meals children will rattle off the grace without thinking about it at all. Shakespeare has two lines about prayer that we should all do well to remember :

"My words fly up, my thoughts remain below,
Words without thoughts never to heaven go."

Dr. Neve and his party reached the town of Leh, the capital of Ladak, and thought it rather a shabby-looking place when they got there. But though it is not grand in appearance it is a busy trading centre, for here come the caravans from India and China, Turkestan and Tibet, and the wares from all these countries are sold in its bazaars on the one broad street that is lined with poplar trees.

Here he met the Moravian missionaries, half a dozen brave men and women quite cut off from the rest of the world, living there in order to give the Gospel to the people of Ladak. A few have become Christians and these, as well as the missionaries, are hoping to be allowed some day to take the Good News into Tibet. Will you not pray that God may change the hearts of the rulers of that country, so that they may no longer close the door to the messengers of Christ?

FAITHFUL UNTO DEATH

WHEN the Lord Jesus was on earth, in a crowd of sick and suffering people, He sometimes asked, "What wilt thou that I should do unto thee?" and more than once the answer came, "Lord, that I might receive my sight."

In the East to-day there are vast numbers of blind people, far more of them than we have here at home. Much blindness is caused by dirt and ignorance, some of it is due to a trouble called cataract. The eye is like a photographic camera, and the front part of the ball is the lens. It is quite transparent. Sometimes it becomes dull and thickened and gradually a person gets blind, but the sight can often be restored by an operation that takes only a few minutes to do. Dr. Neve had the joy of giving sight to hundreds of people at the Srinagar Hospital.

When he was travelling through Little Tibet he saw many blind people in the villages and helped them as far as he was able for he carried his instruments wherever he went.

It was difficult at best, for he had to work in dirty places, or else out of doors.

One night three poor women who had heard his fame came and begged him to give them sight. But it was already dusk and he was camping beside a river, meaning to start before day-break. He told them they must go to Leh, where one of the Moravian missionaries could help them. They could never do that, they said sadly. They could not climb the pass, or get yaks to carry them. As a matter of fact that pass is a good deal higher than Mt. Blanc, so no wonder they dared not attempt it, blind as they were.

The doctor was more than willing to help them but it did not seem possible. However, he told them to come back in the morning and he would see what could be done. Rather than risk missing him, they stayed by the river-side all night. At dawn it was drizzling. You know that in all operations the instruments have to be boiled to kill the germs which usually abound. So the doctor needed a fire, and his carriers tried to light one with flint and steel, but the tinder was moist. One of the Tibetans had a little gunpowder, and put it on a stone, then tore off a bit of his shirt and frayed it out, laid it by the powder and got a spark with the flint and steel. Then they boiled the water in the cooking-pot and the doctor sterilised his instruments.

Next he cleaned the eyes and injected cocaine, as the dentist has very likely done to you before pulling a tooth. Then, kneeling in the sand, he removed the cataracts, and those three women who came blind to the river-side the night before went away seeing. Their joy was too great for words and so also was their gratitude. Surely the doctor was happy, too!

Try and picture the good this man did in a life-time. For him this was not even one morning's work: it was a little job done before breakfast. Would you not love to be a missionary doctor, bringing sight to the blind and health to the sick?

In the Great War both the Neves offered their services. Dr. Arthur was sent first to a large hospital for Indian troops, because he knew their language and understood their ways. Later he was tranferred to a hospital for the German wounded, and he served them as faithfully and kindly as he did the Indians and the British. Then he went over to France and was in one of the foremost clearing stations close to the fighting line, operating on the wounded men while the shells were falling around.

When the War was over he returned to Kashmir and great was the welcome he received. In Mohammedan mosques and Hindu temples people gave thanks for his safe return. High and low alike rejoiced to have him back. Soon he was as busy as ever in his hospital. With the beginning of summer he found himself in the thick of another fight, for cholera broke out in the city. In a short time ten thousand people died. Dr. Neve went up and down the courts and alleys, in and out of the plague-stricken houses, trying to save life and all the while superintending the work of the hospital.

Then at last his strength gave way and after a very short illness he went home to God. When it became known that he had gone, the whole city mourned. They buried him in the little English cemetery, and for a mile and a half the roads were thronged with people who had come to do him honour. British and Indian Christians together carried his coffin, which was draped with the Union Jack. Moslems and Hindus marched twenty abreast in the procession that followed it. In the annals of the city of Srinagar it is recorded of him: " He was truly a doer of golden deeds. Our debt of gratitude to this noble soul is too deep ever to be repaid."

As you think of this hero of the Cross, remember the Lord Jesus has not yet ceased to accept recruits. You also may enrol under His banner if you will. He is ready to make the most and the best of every life that is fully yielded to Him. Can you say from your heart this little verse:

" In full and glad surrender I give myself to Thee,
Thine utterly, and only, and evermore to be:
Oh Son of God, who lovest me, I would be Thine alone,
Let all I have and all I am from henceforth be Thine own."